ASCENDING TO LOVE

Robert Bruce Henley

Copyright © 2012 Robert B. Henley
All Rights Reserved.

No portion of this book may be reproduced without consent of the author.

Servias Ministries Press
P.O. Box 1471
Bethany, OK 73008 U.S.A.
www.servias.org

Manufactured in the United States of America
ISBN: 978-0-615-65752-3

Cover art by Amber R. Nelson
Layout by Sarah Leis

Contents

Preface 3
Introduction 5
Chapter 1 Betraying Love 7
Chapter 2 Gratitude 15
Chapter 3 Dwelling with Our Heavenly Father 22
Chapter 4 Fruitfulness of Love 29
Chapter 5 Love has no opposite 37
Chapter 6 Love Your Enemies 44
Chapter 7 The Consummation of Love 50
Chapter 8 The Eleventh Commandment 56
Chapter 9 The Judgment of Love 61
Chapter 10 The Second Coming of Love 72
Chapter 11 The Unity of Love 79
Chapter 12 The Authority of Love 86
Chapter 13 The Acceptance of Love 94
Chapter 14 The Forgiveness of Love 108
Chapter 15 The Miracles of Love 116
Chapter 16 The Peace of Love 128
Chapter 17 The Choice of Love 139
Chapter 18 Love Compels 149

Preface

The world continues on a path of death and destruction. Unrighteousness fills the airways and we are bombarded with bad news. At this writing, Western civilization has economically overextended itself and the average man has difficulty making ends meet. In many parts of the world information is available on a 24 hour basis by way of the Internet. Global information is growing at an increasing rate but mankind displays the inability to process the information and resolve its problems. There is something missing. The supposed brightest men and women with all of the technology cannot seem to solve the problems plaguing mankind. They assume that they are brighter than the previous generations yet they continue to make the same or similar mistakes in their various attempts toward a solution. Instantaneous communications is not the solution. Ultra high speed computers with massive amounts of storage are not the solution. What is the solution? Where can the solution be found?

Since 2005 I have been compelled to pursue an understanding of the Love of Our Heavenly Father. I have come to realize that if I immerse myself in this study of Love, I will experience positive changes in my life. My loved ones will benefit from this change. There were clearly challenges to this path less taken but confronting those challenges from a position of Love has proven to be right thing to do. Love will have you take actions that are in clear opposition to man's logic and experience. As you trust in Love you will find new opportunities and solutions will open up to you. By converting to Kingdom-based thinking and actions I believe the solutions to mankind's problems will finally be discovered and implemented. There is no unemployment or lack in Heaven. The only way to bring Heaven to earth is by the revelation of Love and responding with action. This book is to encourage you to join me on the path less taken. As we pursue this path we will ascend to Love and bring forth the Kingdom of GOD. Enjoy!

Bob Henley
May, 2012

Introduction

Suppose that I was chosen to receive a revelation from the Throne Room of Heaven. What if from the beginning of time this revelation had been designated for this very hour. Of all the inhabitants of the earth, why would Our Heavenly Father choose me to bring forth a revelation? What if the revelation could change the world but needed someone who would be tenacious in pursuing its fullness. Suppose HE picked the wrong person who would simply sit on the revelation and hide it under a bushel. What if he picked a person who had no access to resources or people who would spread the Word? Why would I write a second book on Love? Wasn't one enough? This book is an expression of Love for mankind and I am compelled by Our Heavenly Father to focus on the self-evident truth that Love is the answer to mankind's problems. Many books are written by storytellers who want to entertain their readers. This is not one of those books. The purpose of this book is to encourage the reader to press in to the revelation of unconditional Love. As we immerse ourselves in Love and its unfathomable attributes we will take on those traits. When this happens we will begin affecting those in our circle of influence. Before long, Love will spread across boundaries and mankind will experience a transformation.

"Come up" is a phrase in Scripture that have tremendous meaning and ramification. Our Heavenly Father called forth Moses to "come up" and receive the Law. John was called to "come up" to the amazing scene in Heaven. My desire is for all of mankind to "come up" to the revelation of Love.

Ascending to Love

There has been a great debate among men concerning free will versus the sovereignty of GOD. Which one is the guiding force? Does man have a choice or does Our Heavenly Father have the plan in place where man cannot change it and we are all simply instruments of the plan? The answer is both and without conflict. The mystery of Love has prevented men from fully understanding that both realities can operate together yet man would have us believe it must be either/or. As we pursue greater revelation of Love, the mystery will unfold and provide peace to man's understanding of Our Heavenly Father's plan. As we gain greater understanding of Love, solutions to the social, political, and economic problems will begin to surface and manifest the new millennium that we all long for as promised in Scripture.

Man can survive in the cause and effect realm by simply mastering the sovereign laws placed into effect to govern this realm. Yes, the sun will rise out of the east tomorrow as it always does. Gravity will play its part as ordained by Our Heavenly Father. The physical laws of the universe were put in place to provide order and structure out of chaos. Mankind has discovered and studied these laws and has generally used these laws for progress. However, there is another yet higher realm of "cause" that has eluded man. The door to that realm requires a key. The door is Jesus and the key is Love. I believe this is the key of David, the man after GOD's own heart. This key will manifest itself as we respond to the call to "come up"!

Chapter 1
Betraying Love

Betrayal involves an act "to deliver" with the connotation of being deceived or given under false pretense. Many of us know the story of Judas betraying Jesus. Judas Iscariot was the treasurer among the disciples and walked with Jesus for the duration of His earthly ministry. Judas, the Greek name for Judah, was believed to have been from a wealthy family and was accustomed to dealing with money and power. The word "Iscariot" contains root words that mean "great men" and "cities" and is tied to Kerioth, a town in the district of Judah. Generally, great men of cities in those times were wealthy giving a second witness to the belief that Judas was indeed from a wealthy family. We also know that wealth can be deceptive in that the wealthy often believe that they were anointed and set apart and above their fellow man endowed with the power of their wealth. Only the wise realize that money has "wings" and place no trust or love in it.

Symbolically, we see by his name Judas is tied to Judah, the fourth son of Jacob. Judah also betrayed the "anointed" of Our Heavenly Father by leading the brothers against Joseph after he had shared his dreams of being exalted. Joseph was seventeen years old at the time, just a kid. Judah was next in line to receive the blessing of Abraham, Isaac, and Jacob was not about to allow his younger brother to get in his way. Judah had operated with the authority of being the elder son and his brothers were easily swayed by his assumed authority. This spirit of entitlement was behind the removal of Joseph from the picture. Judah was not going to compete for the blessing and needed to remove any challenge to his preconceived notion that the blessing could only be given to the next in line. How many times does man think that he needs to help Our Heavenly Father implement the Heavenly Plan? All of Joseph's brothers were willing to betray him for any potential inheritance that might come their way. Greed raised its ugly head among the brothers and motivated them to sacrifice their own flesh and blood. They wanted Joseph removed from their midst. But from a legalistic point of view, they did not want his blood on their hands so they threw him in a pit to die. That plan had risks associated with it so they decided to sell him as a slave for twenty pieces of silver, the number twenty representing "redemption".

This betrayal provided Joseph with the opportunity to go through the cleansing fire. He was a brash teenager at the time and needed maturity before he would operate in his calling. The betrayal by his brothers sent him on a journey that would result in Love saving mankind from a global famine. Joseph's trip to Egypt was designed to change his heart from pride to one of service. Along the way, Joseph received favor and his gifts elevated him in responsibility and authority: "And the LORD was with Joseph, and he was a prosperous man; and he was in the house of his master the Egyptian".

While in Potiphar's employment (Genesis 39), Joseph was betrayed again. Joseph had been sold as a slave to Potiphar, an officer under Pharaoh's command. He had gain favor during his employment and had been elevated to overseer of the house, serving Potiphar. Potiphar's wife lusted after Joseph and when he did not respond, she falsely accused him and handed him over to her husband who promptly put him in prison. This was the second betrayal of a relationship. Betrayal seeks control. However, Love was not to be restricted by man's attempt to control Joseph. Just as life seemed to become bearable, another situation to overcome seems to be placed in our path and our hope and faith that we are truly called is challenged once again.

At the age of eighteen, Joseph is now in prison, the furthest place from his original dream. Things looked worse than when he was thrown in the pit. At least in the pit, he might have some chance of escape. I am sure he had to deal with the emotion of this roller coaster ride he was on. Joseph had to have been an optimist and had that core assurance that Our Heavenly Father would ultimately deliver him once again. As he settled in, the LORD was with Joseph, and showed him mercy, and gave him favor in the sight of the keeper of the prison. Once again, Joseph's gifts and calling were now operational. Men were drawn unto his gifts and responded with placing him in a position of authority. And again Joseph was back to serving, this time in a larger venue. Joseph was now second in command, just under the keeper of the prison. Not a bad position to be in considering it was prison. Anointed by the LORD, everything Joseph set his hand to did prosper. When our gifts are operating properly, we too will prosper. If you are not producing fruit, you must consider the fact that something is blocking your fruitfulness. Are you in the wrong vocation? Are you in habitual lawlessness? Joseph prospered everywhere he went. Adversity will test your calling but fruitfulness will overcome time and time again.

Joseph had settled in as a prisoner with no expectation of freedom. Day after day for ten years, the incarceration continued with no freedom in sight. The original dream had become a distant memory by now. Only by encouraging himself in Our Heavenly Father's Love could he even consider the possibility of his calling to manifest. Little did he know that two more prisoners would be thrust into his life: the baker and the butler, both servants of Pharaoh. They had offended the king and were tossed into prison. It did not take them long to see who really ran the prison. Joseph began serving them as well. Both men had dreams and Joseph received the interpretation from Our Heavenly Father. Our Heavenly Father intervenes to insure you move towards your calling even though it may not manifest immediately. A little bit here and a little bit there. Before long you can look back and see all of the supernatural events that made sure the path to fruition. The baker and the butler were called back to the presence of the king. According to Joseph's interpretation, the butler would be restored and the baker would die. This is exactly what happened. Now, Joseph had a contact close to the king. He surely anticipated an imminent release from prison.

Ascending to Love

According to the Book of Jasher, the butler promised to help Joseph if the dream turned out to be true. The interpretation came to pass and the butler failed to fulfill his promise to Joseph. Once again, man had betrayed Joseph. Joseph's reliance on man for this calling to come to pass had to be removed. Making a deal with the butler was not going to thrust Joseph into his calling. Why? The butler would claim some form of ownership of Joseph's success. If Joseph had immediately been removed from prison based on the butler's intervention, the butler would have attached himself to Joseph's success thus Our Heavenly Father would not have been acknowledged as the source of the fruit. Joseph stayed in prison another two years after the restoration of the butler, enough time for any claim to Joseph's calling to be eliminated.

Joseph had two years to dwell on the fact that man would not facilitate his calling. Once again he realized that trusting in the LORD would be his only path to fulfilling the dream at the age of seventeen. Now that he had learned that lesson, the plan continued. The king dreamed two dreams and nobody in the kingdom could interpret them. In his own self interest, the butler saw his chance to gain favor with the king. He knew that Joseph was anointed by Our Heavenly Father to interpret dreams with great precision. This would insure his continued employment for life.

Joseph had to ascend seventy steps to address Pharaoh. Each step represented a different language Joseph had to speak in order to ascend to a higher level. With the help of an angel the night before, he learned the seventy known languages which enabled him to speak to Pharaoh face to face. His call to service came to fruition on that day. He had been in a severe training program to remove his ego-driven attitude in order that he would serve mankind through Love. Joseph was betrayed by his brothers, Potiphar's wife, and the king's butler but none of those betrayals would prevent Our Heavenly Father's plan from being completed. Joseph learned how to serve and be under authority. His immaturity had to be removed and replaced with wisdom and understanding. His story included suffering, failures, betrayals, and lies but in the end his calling of Love prevailed.

Absalom was King David's third son. He was described as the most handsome man and without blemish and I am sure that he loved to be reminded of that fact. This gift of beauty fed his ego to the point of betraying his father. Is there anything worse than being betrayed by your son or daughter? Absalom's ego demanded power without regard for the law. David's oldest son Amnon had been lovesick over Tamar, his half-sister. He plotted a way to get her into his bed and he raped her. Absalom was determined to get revenge even though it was not his responsibility to carry out judgment. He took matters in his own hand and killed Amnon, the first-born of the king. David mourned for Amnon but after three years longed to see Absalom. Finally, Absalom was restored to his father David but lived towards the gate of the city. He craftily used his position to gain the loyalty of the people of Israel by claiming to be an impartial judge on all matter of dispute. Once he had gained widespread loyalty, he betrayed his father.

Men will try to remove you from your calling. Their self-interest will scheme and plot ways to get ahead and will betray anyone who gets in the way of their goal. They may use Scripture to justify their actions, out of context of course. They may use "the Word of the Lord" to sway you into submitting to their plan. Loved ones will do the same especially due to the fact they know your emotional weaknesses toward them. They will manipulate you into enabling their lawless plan. If you fail to respond, betrayal is not far from their minds.

As you focus on dealing with the betrayal, your time and energy is diverted away from your calling. You wake up one day and realize that you have done nothing concerning your calling for weeks or months. In looking back to determine why, you suddenly realize that the betrayal or betrayals consumed your time, money, resources, and focus. This is why it is important to understand betrayal and not allow it to steal you away from your calling. As you move closer to Our Heavenly Father, HE will reveal the hearts of those you are dealing with. When you discern the intent of those whom you have dealings with, you are able to remove yourself from their midst. If you cannot trust someone, why would you want to have further fellowship or business dealings with them even though the promise of success

Ascending to Love

appears to be imminent? Don't you think that Our Heavenly Father can bring forth another business deal of even greater opportunity? Do you think that the "friend" who is untrustworthy is the last friend you will have? Fellowshipping with lawlessness and betrayal is dangerous. Before you know it you are swept into their sin and become associated with it.

Finally, we must direct this betrayal towards the mirror. The ultimate betrayer is within us. Our flesh or ego has been a force to reckon with. This master manipulator within us will stop at nothing to control our every move and thought. In Colossians 3:5:

> Put to death, therefore, whatever belongs to your earthly nature: sexual immorality, impurity, lust, evil desires and greed, which is idolatry. (NIV)

Can any among us claim exception to this list of earthly nature? Our "earthly nature" aka ego, operates with great subtlety and would blind us to its devices in order that it can maintain control over our every thought. But we are told to take every thought captive. We are to put to death those thoughts, habits, assumptions, and actions that belong to our earthly nature. We are to ascend to a higher level. We must put to death those fleshly desires and clean our earthen vessel of the sin and lawlessness that has crept in. Some of these sins have been generational in nature. As we grow older, we can see the subtle impact of our ancestors on our way of thinking. We must be released from this bondage and Love is the bond breaker. Paul explains in Romans 6:12:

> Therefore do not let sin reign in your mortal body, that you should obey it in its lusts. (NKJV)

"Therefore do not" means that we have command over this mortal body that wants to betray us. The flesh would have us believe that immediate self-gratification is worth the sacrifice of our gifts and our calling. But once the gratification is gone, we are left with emptiness and guilt. The next time this self-gratification raises its ugly head, the need to satisfy is even greater and requires more. Before long, an addiction has manifested that requires constant gratification. I would suggest that every addict started out without the knowledge that the first move that led to the addiction would have the ramification thereof. Addiction comes in all flavors: drugs, alcohol, tobacco, cola, caffeine, sex, emotional, video games, internet, religiosity, power, apparent prophetic signs, etc. Anything that gratifies the flesh and creates a predisposed focus when it is absent from you is an addiction. When you find yourself plotting to get satisfaction from a particular substance or action, you are being betrayed. The focus of time and/or resources is meant to move you away from your calling in a most subtle and crafty way. We must be open and transparent with ourselves and expose the ego for what it is. We must be vigilant to mortify our flesh and walk in the Spirit.

> Romans 6:19 I speak in human terms because of the weakness of your flesh. For just as you presented your members as slaves of uncleanness, and of lawlessness leading to more lawlessness, so now present your members as slaves of righteousness for holiness. (NKJV)

Each of us has the authority and responsibility to present our members as servants of righteousness for holiness. Our bodies are going to serve either sin or Love, there is no middle ground of nothingness. "How can I do this?" you would ask. You have moved so far from the Throne of GOD you are in the outer darkness and it looks pretty bleak. The Spirit of GOD is everywhere. There is no place where you can't be found and restored, Love makes sure of that. Love comes to you and draws you closer to Our Heavenly Father. We have all betrayed Our Heavenly Father at some point in our lives and probably more often than any of us would like to admit. If this was not such a big issue, the Apostle Paul would not have devoted so much writing to this aspect of our lives. Paul writes in Ephesians:

5:11 And have no fellowship with the unfruitful works of darkness, but rather expose them. (NKJV)

As we expose those unfruitful works and repent of them, our cleansing begins. A fact of life is that "we become like the company we keep". We must no longer fellowship with those who would steer us away from righteous living. You cannot hang out with a drug dealer and expect to overcome your addiction. On the other hand, when you immerse yourself in Scriptures of Love you become Love. When you dwell and meditate on Our Heavenly Father and HIS Love, you become Love. When you act as Our Lord Jesus Christ acted in the Scripture, you become Love. As your focus becomes Love your calling begins to manifest and the betrayer becomes history.

Personal Assessment:
1. Make a list of those who you have betrayed.
2. Have you ask them for forgiveness?
3. Why did you betray them?
4. If Jesus appeared to you now, would you reasons hold up?
5. Have you betrayed an immediate family member? Why?

Chapter 2
Gratitude

Gratitude is the key to the heart. Why do we pray over our food? Many people these days would say they were raised by their parents to say a prayer before each meal. Giving thanks for your meal is meant to be an expression of gratitude. We should maintain an attitude of gratitude at all times. In the United States we celebrate Thanksgiving each year. It often includes turkey, dressing, mashed potatoes, and pumpkin pie. This custom is to remember the pilgrims giving thanks unto Our Heavenly Father for sustaining them after their arrival to the New World. Often revelation simply becomes a custom over time. All of us should focus on the revelation that produced the tradition and renew ourselves each and every day.

The basic necessities of life include food, shelter, and clothing. Those who have never had to worry about these necessities tend to form an attitude of entitlement. This is the beginning of their downfall. The ego would have us believe that our gifts and calling entitle us to certain benefits above and beyond the rest of humanity. This exalted view of ourselves is an attempt to create a division between us and the rest of humanity. Eventually we become arrogant and expect everyone else to bow to our every need and begin to act as though we should be served by others rather than the opposite. Any blemish or flaw is covered up by our pride and we try to project an air of superiority. We focus our time and money on creating the perception of perfection while alienating our friends and loved ones. The time and money would have been better spent meeting their needs and serving them.

Let's face it, "This is the day that the LORD hath made" and we had nothing to do with it! Our Heavenly Father needed no assistance or input by us to put this universe together. In this ever-expanding universe, the earth is just a speck and within that speck you and I reside. As we look toward the night sky and dwell upon the vastness of creation, our attitude should turn from entitlement to gratitude.

"I will praise the LORD according to his righteousness" is spoken by the psalmist. Our Heavenly Father is the One who deserves thanksgiving and praise. By speaking this forth on a daily basis, we are reminded of our relative position in life. HE is GOD, not us. Love gives honor where honor is due and in a righteous fashion. It is not wrong to express appreciation to those who have done good works but thanksgiving and praise is reserved for The Creator of the universe. Undo focus on individuals tends to feed their egos and they start believing they deserve the accolades without any help from Above.

Wealth tends to promote self-gratification. When a person is in a position of wealth, he believes he is special and anointed to be exalted. Frequently he expects more wealth should be channeled his way and the subtlety of greed sets in. As greed settles in, evil now has a fertile ground to produce bad fruit or no fruit at all. The GOD given gifts are used for self promotion rather than to serve mankind. Gratitude becomes a distant memory. Often he will mask his greed by projecting a willingness to give it all up but expecting to never to be poor again.

Extreme adversity brings forth gratitude. Greed creeps in slowly and unnoticed over an extended period of time. Compromise takes over and the principles that allowed the gifts to operate in a Godly manner dissipate into distant memory. Time passes and the wealthy person finds it necessary to bend the rules to keep the cash flowing. First, it is a minor "white" lie. But later this person expands the lawlessness and begins to use the legal system to exploit the weakness of the business adversary. No longer is the person living by the "spirit" of the law but now only by the letter of the law and all of its exceptions. Charitable contributions listed on the tax return began to disappear. One by one flaws are found in the charitable organizations that justify withholding any further donations. Life becomes more complex. Now the wealthy person must track everything said to all business associates to insure a legal position can be sustained when adversity arises, and it will. The focus and energy to maintain this false kingdom ultimately fails and the collapse arrives, often from an unexpected and uncontrollable event. Jesus warns the rich in His Sermon on the Mount:

> Luke 6:24   But woe unto you that are rich! for ye have received your consolation

Jesus warns the rich that grief will arrive soon. He reveals the final outcome of their wealth:

> 25   Woe unto you that are full! for ye shall hunger. Woe unto you that laugh now! for ye shall mourn and weep.
> 26   Woe unto you, when all men shall speak well of you! for so did their fathers to the false prophets. (KJV)

Only after the wealth has been removed will the wealthy person become desperate and return to Our Heavenly Father. Yes, there will be some form of corrective judgment but it will be done in Love. There will be lost opportunity to be a blessing that the wealth could have provided. In the biggest of pictures, Our Heavenly Father allowed for this missed opportunity by the wealthy person. Another steward was being raised up as this steward was moving toward the outer darkness. Heaven will not be denied its plan. When the formerly wealthy person is stripped of all the money and its attachments, clarity arrives and Love enters in. Gratitude replaces greed. Humbleness replaces arrogance. It was a costly training exercise but a necessary outcome to root out the greed in the heart. How many prodigal sons do we need to meet before we finally get the picture? Focus on true gratitude for your daily bread and leave no entrance for greed to infiltrate your heart.

After the warning to the rich, Jesus discloses proper stewardship principles for all to live by:

27   But I say unto you which hear, Love your enemies, do good to them which hate you,

Unconditional Love will convert an enemy and hate cannot stand up to this Love. Hatred needs an adversary in order to thrive. Hate is aggressive and without an external enemy to direct its energy, hatred will consume itself. Nations with adversaries would be wise to consider the wisdom of this Word.

28   Bless them that curse you, and pray for them which despitefully use you.

Let's face it. Everyone gets cursed by another and despitefully used. As long as arrogance and the attitude of entitlement are found among us, we will get an opportunity to respond with many prayers and blessings.

29   And unto him that smiteth thee on the [one] cheek offer also the other; and him that taketh away thy cloke forbid not [to take thy] coat also.

Those who would test your heart by provoking a response from you will receive an unexpected reaction- Love. Hatred needs justification to perpetuate its energy. Love will dissipate that energy and evoke remorse instead.

30   Give to every man that asketh of thee; and of him that taketh away thy goods ask [them] not again.

In the world there are givers and takers. If you have resources, be willing to help those in need. Ask Our Heavenly Father whether to give and how much. Obviously you cannot meet every need of those who cross your path. That is why it is so important that we be sensitive to Our Heavenly Father's voice when HE sends someone for us to bless. One of the most difficult things our flesh deals with is the judgment of the person whom we gave money. Our flesh wants to judge the actions and habits of that person. It is critical to understand that our blessing comes from our obedience and intent, not the other person's actions or outcome!

> 31 And as ye would that men should do to you, do ye also to them likewise.

The Golden Rule is the outworking of Unconditional Love. What an easy barometer to use when dealing with others in a business transaction. How brief would business contracts become when this Truth is the guiding principle contained in the contract. The legal profession would shrink and the courts would no longer be overrun with litigation cases. Businesses would simply "do the right thing" by their customers, suppliers, investors, and employees. Manipulation and exploitation would be replaced with Truth and blessing, fruits of Love.

> 32 For if ye love them which love you, what thank have ye? for sinners also love those that love them.
> 33 And if ye do good to them which do good to you, what thank have ye? for sinners also do even the same.
> 34 And if ye lend [to them] of whom ye hope to receive, what thank have ye? for sinners also lend to sinners, to receive as much again.

Conditional love has self-gratification in the midst of it. Jesus conveys the fact that it is difficult to differentiate loved ones from sinners by their actions. Anyone can act accordingly in a conditional relationship. The conditions set forth and expected will ultimately result in a failure to perform for none of us are perfect. This relationship will be filled with tension and judgment. The stronger person will evoke a divisive and elevated position over the weaker. Over time, the weaker one will develop resentment and bitterness toward the stronger one. Unconditional Love must then enter into the relationship

Ascending to Love

in order to remove this root of bitterness. Otherwise, death of the relationship will occur.

Jesus sums up the right approach for those who have been given the privilege of being stewards with a few simple directives that reflect the heart and character of Our Heavenly Father:

> 35   But love ye your enemies, and do good, and lend, hoping for nothing again; and your reward shall be great, and ye shall be the children of the Highest: for he is kind unto the unthankful and [to] the evil.

Do you want to be known as a "child of the Highest"? Then do the words of Jesus! Take on the character of Our Heavenly Father, the GOD of Love. Further:

> 36   Be ye therefore merciful, as your Father also is merciful.
> 37   Judge not, and ye shall not be judged: condemn not, and ye shall not be condemned: forgive, and ye shall be forgiven:

In the above passage, Jesus succinctly directs our focus to the realities of acceptable stewardship and provides us the Heavenly perspective of true stewardship in the area of relationships, distribution expectations, dealing with adversaries, and setting the standard for the child of the Highest. As we operate according to those directives, only then we can then expect the following:

> Luke 6:38   Give, and it shall be given unto you; good measure, pressed down, and shaken together, and running over, shall men give into your bosom. For with the same measure that ye mete withal it shall be measured to you again. (KJV)

Many Christians in the "faith" movement latched on to this verse as a path toward financial prosperity. The problem is that many failed to read and understand the previous verses that provide the conditions by which you could expect men to give into your bosom. Our Heavenly Father is in the multiplication business. As HIS stewards walk according to unconditional Love, their resources will be multiplied for greater service. For those who walk according to their own lusts, what they have will be taken away.

As we understand these Heavenly principles, we can truly be grateful for our station in life no matter how great or small. An attitude of gratitude sets that stage for us to be used in a greater manner by Our Heavenly Father. We need to keep this reality before us daily!

Personal Assessment:
1. When did you last express gratitude to a loved one?
2. When did you last express gratitude to a stranger?
3. Look out the window. Is there something there for you to express gratitude to our Heavenly Father?
4. Make a point to express heartfelt gratitude to another person at least one per day.
5. Write a note to someone and express gratitude for their existence.

Chapter 3
Dwelling with Our Heavenly Father

*F*ellowship with Our Heavenly Father is the highest level of relationship a person can have. What more could one ask for than to have an intimate relationship with the Creator of Heaven and earth. We all desire fellowship with others and have a deep seated need to be loved. Those who have been hurt by loved ones in the past will build walls of protection only to find those walls become a prison of isolation and agony. They had been vulnerable to their loved ones only to be used and exploited for selfish reasons. On the other hand, Our Creator who is the GOD of Love has only our best interest at heart. There are many mysteries we cannot comprehend but Our Heavenly Father has full understanding and will guide us through those mysteries in His lovingkindness, grace, and mercy.

Moses was given a pattern to follow to enable Our Heavenly Father to dwell with the children of Israel. The Tabernacle in the wilderness provides us with a simple understanding of "dwelling in His Presence":

> Exodus 25:8-9 And let them make me a sanctuary; that I may dwell among them, According to all that I show you, that is, the pattern of the tabernacle and the pattern of all its furnishings, just so you shall make it. (NKJV)

Thus Our Heavenly Father gives us a pattern by which we can expect His Glory to dwell among us or in us as our Tabernacle is now our body. Moses was given elaborate and detailed instructions for the design of the Tabernacle and its contents, each detail being symbolic bursting with meaning. Further instructions were given for the lawful entrance into the Holy of Holies by the priest. There were three basic steps to bring forth the Glory of Our Heavenly Father:

1 Draw near unto Yahweh.

Lev 9:5-6   And they brought [that] which Moses commanded before the tabernacle of the congregation: and all the congregation drew near and stood before the LORD.
And Moses said, This [is] the thing which the LORD commanded that ye should do: and the glory of the LORD shall appear unto you.

2 Present sacrifices to THE LORD

There were two types of sacrifices: sin and gift offerings. Once the sin offerings had dealt with the "flesh", gift offerings were given as a sweet smelling savor to Our Heavenly Father.

Lev 9:7-22
3 Bless the people

Lev 9:23   And Moses and Aaron went into the tabernacle of the congregation, and came out, and blessed the people: and the glory of the LORD appeared unto all the people

This pattern was an external type and shadow of bringing forth the Glory of GOD. Until Jesus became flesh and fulfilled the five types of sacrifices, the priests were charged with ministering to Our Heavenly Father with the pattern mentioned above. Once Jesus satisfied the requirement of the Levitical sacrifice, He provided all of us with the opportunity to "draw near" unto Our Heavenly Father.

Bringing forth the Glory, the anointing, the power of Our Heavenly Father among us requires reverence and respect. When the Glory appeared, the people fell on their face (Lev 9:24). The Glory

Ascending to Love

is greater than all of mankind yet man is so self-centered he fails to comprehend the need for reverence.

Paul understood this pattern when he wrote:

Draw near:
Hebrews 10:22 Let us draw near with a true heart in full assurance of faith, having our hearts sprinkled from an evil conscience, and our bodies washed with pure water.

Present the sacrifices:
Romans 12:1 I beseech you therefore, brethren, by the mercies of God, that ye present your bodies a living sacrifice, holy, acceptable unto God, [which is] your reasonable service.

Bless the people:
Roman 12:14 Bless them which persecute you: bless, and curse not.

In Romans 12, Paul provides us with much detail on how to bless others and specifically: 12:9 Let love be without hypocrisy. Abhor what is evil. Cling to what is good. If you want the Glory of GOD to flow through you, Love must be the motivating force in your actions.

At the core of our soul is a deep-seated insecurity of abandonment by Our Heavenly Father, a point of separation. When man left the garden of Eden, his glory had left him. It has been mathematically shown that Adam was 33 ½ years old when the glory departed. This separation has been transmitted through the body water of the sperm and egg ever since. Intelligent memory can be isolated in "God" particles, the smallest particle in the universe. This memory is a carrier of instruction and knowledge, both positive and negative. When the sins of the father are mentioned in Scripture, the knowledge and propensity to sin are transmitted by these carriers. This is true of disease, chemical exposure, and germ exposure as well. Our ancestors were exposed to syphilis in the late 1800's and the outworking in later generations is cancer. This syphilis wave form acts as a catalyst for the formation and reproduction of cancer cells. Emotional states can be transmitted as well. This abandonment is reinforced by our earthly parents no matter how well they performed in our childhood.

This perceived separation is further enforced by our ego's desire for control. "I am on my own and nobody really cares about me or my future." We begin to believe the lie and begin to think Our Heavenly Father is some harsh taskmaster just waiting to bust us over the head with a big stick. We are introduced to the Old Testament and with immature eyes see a harsh God who is punishing the children of Israel at every turn. We see armies wiped out in an instant. Who is this Creator who would kill all those people? Our narrow perspective would tell us that life is finished at physical death for we have yet to understand infinity. We don't understand that our spirit does not die but lives forever with Our Creator. But as we mature in our understanding and wisdom, we begin to see the panoramic view of life. As we have children, we see the necessity of correction and the rod of punishment. Compliance is required for the safety of the child even though the parent's motive of protection is not understood. A fear of authority is maintained until the child comes of age and understands the need for laws to insure safety and fruitfulness.

This separation must be exposed and dealt with. When you begin to pursue the revelation of Love you will see the intent by which you were separated. Cell division is required for growth in the body just as a "division" is required for multiplication of the Kingdom, somewhat of a paradox. When you left your mother's womb you were separated so that you could grow and fulfill your own calling. Our Heavenly Father placed the desire for restoration and communion inside of you at conception. That emptiness demanded fulfillment but many have tried to fill it with worldly solutions: drugs, alcohol, or other addictions. Each addiction could only provide a temporary satisfaction but soon the craving for fulfillment demanded more.

We are told to "Draw near". Our Heavenly Father is the center of all of creation. His Throne is immovable and is pure in every aspect and sin has no place before this most Holy Place. The Blood of Jesus

Ascending to Love

Christ cleanses us of our sin and allows us to draw near unto Our Heavenly Father. Our ego would have us believe we are unworthy to stand before the Creator of Heaven and earth. In order to draw near we must quiet our ego and be assured that our Savior satisfied the requirement for us to move into the intimate relationship our soul so deeply desires.

As we expose ourselves to Our Heavenly Father and become open and transparent with HIM, we begin to take on HIS attributes of Love. Just as a boy emulates his father, we begin to see the attributes of Love in Our Heavenly Father and desire to act in the same manner. No longer do we see the person who wants to harm us as an enemy but instead see a hurting soul without understanding. Rather than fuel the fire that would sustain the enemy, we begin to respond out of Love and compassion. Our priorities begin to change and those things that were once important to our flesh no longer have any control over us. Those addictive cravings are replaced with desires to be a blessing.

Love gives. Once we have drawn near to our Heavenly Father, we will then present ourselves as a sacrifice. "Use me, Father" will be our innermost desire. Our trepidation is replaced by anticipation. Our Heavenly Father begins to reveal our true reality. The misconceived emotion that we are unacceptable and cannot come boldly to the Throne of Grace is our ego attempting to prolong the division it promotes in order to maintain control. Our Heavenly Father longs for our presence before HIS Face. Just as a parent who takes great pride in seeing his or her child graduate from school, Our Heavenly Father rejoices in our graduation from the immature who is tutored by the Law to the mature who is now above the Law and no longer needs the Law to insure a righteous walk.

John 10:30   I and [my] Father are one. (KJV)

Jesus made this unequivocal statement when asked by the Jews, "Are you the Christ?" Jesus' response enraged the Jews to pick up stones to stone him. When I say that my wife and I are one, nobody has a problem in understanding that we fellowship, have intimacy, discuss our plans, and are accountable to one another. The Jews were unable to consider that Jesus had a relationship even above that of Moses or Abraham. They could not conceive that someone in their midst could claim such a close relationship. It is clear that they did not have or conceive of the possibility of such a closeness to Our Heavenly Father. Jesus is our example and consistently directs us to a relationship with Our Heavenly Father as an elder brother should. Jesus said, "I am the door." He is the door to what? The door is a passage to the presence of Our Heavenly Father. The door is not the destination in itself but the path to the destination. Jesus began this truth by the following statement:

> John 10:1 "Most assuredly, I say to you, he who does not enter the sheepfold by the door, but climbs up some other way, the same is a thief and a robber. 2 But he who enters by the door is the shepherd of the sheep. 3 To him the doorkeeper opens, and the sheep hear his voice; and he calls his own sheep by name and leads them out. (NKJV)

The facts are as follows:
- The sheep are in the courtyard, behind a wall of protection.
- The courtyard has a lawful entrance: the door.
- The doorkeeper has a key to open the door to allow rightful passage.
- The thief and the robber will climb the wall to bypass the proper entry.
- The sheep can and do hear His voice.
- He calls the sheep by name to lead them out

The mere fact you are reading this would indicate that you are one of the sheep. The fact that your name is known indicates there is some type of fellowship already. There is a wall of protection but it can be overtaken by lawlessness and Jesus provides us a perspective of how serious this lawlessness can be:

> John 10:10 The thief cometh not, but for to steal, and to kill, and to destroy: I am come that they might have life, and that they might have [it] more abundantly. (KJV)

Jesus came that we might have life and the fullness thereof. We must pass through the door with the Key of David. Love brought Jesus to the earth, Love opens the door, and Love is inside the door waiting for us to embrace it that we might have it more abundantly. As we embrace Love, the prime characteristic of Our Heavenly Father, we are dwelling with HIM.

Personal Assessment:
1. Get to a quiet place with no distractions and simply express your gratitude to Our Heavenly Father.
2. Think of several acts of Our Heavenly Father mentioned in Scripture and discover the motivation of Love behind those acts.
3. Look for Our Heavenly Father in a loved one.
4. Read only the words of Jesus in Scripture. He spoke only what Our Heavenly Father directed Him to speak.

Chapter 4
FRUITFULNESS OF LOVE

When people see you, do they see Jesus or do they just see another person in search of fulfillment? Do they come knocking on your door for you to lay hands on the sick? What is missing from our walk with Our Heavenly Father? Action.

Christians have a tendency to believe that if they don't operate in one of the nine Spiritual Gifts listed in 1 Corinthians, they have no ministry to fulfill. Wrong. Paul writes to Timothy concerning those who have wealth:

> 1 Timothy 6:17 Command those who are rich in this present age not to be haughty, nor to trust in uncertain riches but in the living God, who gives us richly all things to enjoy.
> 18 Let them do good, that they be rich in good works, ready to give, willing to share,
> 19 storing up for themselves a good foundation for the time to come, that they may lay hold on eternal life.

The United States is the wealthiest country on earth and our poor are generally wealthier than most who live in third world countries. We are to do good and be rich in good works, not idly set in a pew or recliner and endlessly analyze the Scriptures to tickle our minds. We often look beyond the needs in our own backyard and focus on the needs in another state or country. Why not distribute to both?

Are you ready to give and willing to share? There must be balance in giving and sharing. A farmer does not eat the seed he plans to plant next season. You don't give you rent money to a ministry or

Ascending to Love

fail to make your house payment. You need to honor your word, and that includes contracts you have signed. Are you hoarding? If so, that is a symptom of an unwillingness to share. Bless those who are less fortunate with your excess clothing and other goods. Do we really need all those storage rentals?

Paul indicates that good works, ready to give, and willing to share provide a good foundation for eternal life. These are good fruit produced by Love. Paul further expresses characteristics of Love in Romans 12:

> 9   Let love be without hypocrisy. Abhor what is evil. Cling to what is good.
> 10   Be kindly affectionate to one another with brotherly love, in honor giving preference to one another;

Love lives what it proclaims. Love does not say one thing and do another in deceitfulness Love is sincere and hates evil and what it does to people. Love overcomes evil with good and is devoted to others and honors them, their unique gifts and calling.

Love is "zealous" by being diligent to all things Our Heavenly Father brings forth to be dealt with. As we walk in our calling, our passion to serve mankind in our calling motivates us to get up in the morning and be excited to what the day will bring. Depression has no place in a person motivated by Love. Depression has its roots in the ego of the person who is not in control but cannot see the gifts and calling bestowed on him or her. May the eyes of our understanding be opened that we may see the calling bestowed on each of us before we were formed in the womb!

When we walk in Love, we are rejoicing in hope and patient in tribulation for we know that Love has overcome the world and all its obstacles. We know that Our Heavenly Father's resources are at our direction to bring forth the fullness of our calling. Every particle in the universe, including every particle in our body, is at the command of Love. Those "GOD" particles that are needed for our calling await our Love-filled words to come forth and manifest on our behalf. Good fruit forms along our life's path as an outworking of the evidence of our Love.

As our fruit abounds, our relationship with Our Heavenly Father becomes more intimate. Hearing HIS voice is no longer difficult or questioned for the fruit is a constant confirmation and witness to our soul that we have become that connection between Heaven and earth. People begin to see us as HIS personal representative rather than just another voice in the noise of humanity. We look forward to those quiet times when Our Heavenly Father gives us direction for the day, peace for our soul, and the assurance that all obstacles will be overcome.

As the fruit in our account abounds in Love, we look forward to distributing to the needs of the saints and we are given to hospitality. Our house becomes a welcomed stop for travelers like a cool drink in the desert. Babies will take long naps in the bedroom because they perceive the peace in the house. They utilize their ability to discern auras and when they see you, they smile and enjoy the comfort of being held by you. Not every saint has been given the gift of finances and those who have been give the gift are to distribute to those who haven't for each member of the Body of Christ is called to supply others with his or her fruitfulness.

Persecutions will come but instead of promoting an adversarial relationship, we bless the instigator of such persecutions rather than speak curses over them. With blessing comes cleansing and correction by Our Heavenly Father for it is written, ""Vengeance is Mine, I will repay," says the Lord."

In your fellowship with others, take part in their lives, both the ups and the downs. Do not set yourself above another but find common ground to establish a relationship. Jesus did not hesitate to set at the table with sinners. The servers at the restaurants you frequent have a calling from Our Heavenly Father and need encouragement from time to time. Find out one fact about their life and show them your sincerity for their wellbeing.

Another fruit of Love is harmony and we should pursue a life and a walk of restoration rather than division. If we are to be righteous judges, we cannot be "high-minded" but must view every individual with the same Love and respect no matter what their station of life. Yes the rich and wealthy need ministry but so do the downtrodden and poor. Our list of friends should not exclude either group.

As I grow older, I place less value on my opinion, claiming to be wiser than the other person in the conversation. As long as the wisdom is from above I can confidently and boldly proclaim a truth. However, when the opinion comes from my soul it is subject to judgment which can sometimes reap harsh results. If we stop and reflect on some of our past opinions, we would prefer to take those words back and flush them down the toilet. "What was I thinking?"

Love does not produce "evil" fruit. The word "evil" is found 613 times in the King James Version, one for every law and statute in the Old Testament. Evil is destructive and injurious whereas Love is creative and restorative in nature. When judging fruit you should view the result of the action and determine which category the action can be classified. When evil is directed towards you, how do you respond? Do you move towards restoration or destruction? Do you create an adversary or attempt to reconcile? What is your reputation? Are you known to do what is right in the sight of all men?

If it is possible, as much as depends on you, live peaceably with all men. This can be a challenge especially in a country that thrives on the paradigm of creating enemies. An enemy is created by division, it's us against them; you are either for us or against us; it is "my way or the highway". The ego wants to maintain control of you so that you don't walk by the Spirit. In pursuing that control, the ego needs an enemy, a division that requires time and energy to direct your focus and preoccupy you with tasks that remove you from your calling. Your gifts are used to pursue destruction rather than creation. Time is wasting away and your calling lies dormant while you deal with the evil of the day. Your focus is now to be victorious over the enemy and at the end of this vicious cycle, the result is emptiness. Yes, you may be able to tell the other person "I told you so" but in the meantime you have lost a potential friend, destroyed a relationship, or deferred the other person from fulfilling their calling.

How should evil be repaid? "Vengeance is mine, I will repay" says Our Heavenly Father. HE created the universe and all its laws in a state of equilibrium. Both blessing and cursing are a result of the equilibrium being maintained. As you pursue Love, the universe responds in its creative attributes of blessing. But if you pursue evil, lawlessness, and sin, the universe responds with cursing. Whether active or passive, the result is assured.

All of the universe is created by Our Heavenly Father and reflects HIS character of Love. HIS laws also reflect HIS character. Love will not reward lawlessness nor promote it. By pursuing the revelation of Love and walking in it, you open yourself up to the blessings of the universe and its contents. Witty inventions are waiting on the right intent to unlock the revelation that will benefit both you and all of those who are affected by your invention. New methods of conservation are waiting in the Heavenly realm for the person motivated by Love to bring forth these methods. Do you think that only evil men are successful? Their success is only temporal for their motivation arose from greed. Our Heavenly Father has used "heathens" to bring forth new inventions ordained for specific times. Those inventions could just as easily been brought forth by righteous men but they were not pursuing Love. In the biggest of pictures, Our Heavenly Father's plan will come forth even if HE needs to use a heathen to implement it. We are shown this in Isaiah 45 verse 1:

> "Thus saith the LORD to his anointed, to Cyrus, whose right hand I have holden, to subdue nations before him"

Cyrus was the king of Persia and conqueror of Babylon; first ruler of Persia to make a decree allowing the Israelite exiles to return to Jerusalem. He was not among the "chosen people" of Israel. This Scripture makes it perfectly clear that Our Heavenly Father will anoint whomever HE desires to bring forth HIS plan. Israel would sin greatly thus bringing forth a curse over the nation to be implemented by Our Heavenly Father's "anointed". You may have been called by Our Heavenly Father to do great and mighty things but if you are lawless you will be under judgment and repayment is demanded. The judgment may be reduced by the grace and mercy of Our Heavenly Father but habitual lawlessness will reap death and destruction.

> Genesis 1:11 And God said, Let the earth bring forth grass, the herb yielding seed, [and] the fruit tree yielding fruit after his kind, whose seed [is] in itself, upon the earth: and it was so. (KJV)

Out of HIS character of Love, Our Heavenly Father spoke the Law of Fruitfulness into being. An apple seed will only produce an apple. A rabbit will produce only rabbits, possibly more than you might want. This is a powerful law. Genetics is subject to this law and each fruit tree will only produce after its own kind. The fruit tree is designed to sustain its kind by generating and multiplying seed to insure its survival. If an oak tree is stressed in the summer, expect a bumper crop of acorns in the fall for it is simply responding to the words of Love spoken in Genesis 1:11.

> Genesis 1: 12 And the earth brought forth grass, [and] herb yielding seed after his kind, and the tree yielding fruit, whose seed [was] in itself, after his kind: and God saw that [it was] good.

Love stuck around to insure the manifestation of the Law responded properly. Once set in motion, the universe adheres to the Laws of Creation. Our Heavenly Father watches over His creation in a state of rest or equilibrium. HE is not wringing His hands hoping that the earth will not fall out of orbit. The universe is designed to maintain equilibrium and will respond as needed to restore equilibrium. If a law of the universe is broken, a judgment of corrective action will immediately respond and restore balance.

Genesis 8:22 While the earth remaineth, seedtime and harvest, and cold and heat, and summer and winter, and day and night shall not cease. (KJV)

As long as the earth exists, there is planting of seed and harvesting of fruit. That is a law you can bank on! Unlike man's law, these laws will last eons without variance. In Psalms 112, the righteous man is described:

> Who delights greatly in His commandments.
> His descendants will be mighty on earth;
> He will be blessed.
> Wealth and riches will be in his house,
> And his righteousness endures forever.
> Unto the upright there arises light in the darkness;
> He is gracious, and full of compassion, and righteous.
> He deals graciously and lends;
> He will guide his affairs with discretion.
> He will never be shaken;
> He will be in everlasting remembrance.
> He will not be afraid of evil tidings;
> His heart is steadfast, trusting in the LORD.
> His heart is established;
> He will not be afraid.

In Matthew 13, Jesus speaks forth the parable of the sower. He is referring to Genesis 1:11 in that there is no question whether good seed will produce good fruit. The issue here is the interference of evil to the production of the fruit. The translators externalized the interference by adding the word "one" to the Scripture.

> Matthew 13:19 "When anyone hears the word of the kingdom, and does not understand it , then the wicked one comes and snatches away what was sown in his heart."

Jesus simply said "the wicked" comes, not wicked one. This word's root meaning is: 1) great trouble, intense desire 2) pain. I would suggest the source of this "wicked" is your ego wanting to maintain control rather than assigning an external being a god-like power equivalent to Our Heavenly Father that can be omnipresent to deal out great trouble to millions of Christians. When we pursue a life to bring forth good fruit, WE WILL BE TESTED! It will not occur without trials and temptations. In order to be an overcomer, you must overcome something. Jesus tells us that our seed must be planted in good ground. We are told to protect ourselves from the seductiveness of wealth. Greed will choke out the Word of God and you will bear no fruit.

Paul shares in Romans 12 the actions Love takes, "If your enemy is hungry, feed him; If he is thirsty, give him a drink; for in so doing you will heap coals of fire on his head." Most of all, do not be overcome by evil, but overcome evil with good.

Personal Assessment:
1. Make a list of your "fruit" over the last 30 days.
2. Make a list of the fruit you would like to produce in your life.
3. Locate Scriptures that support the fruit you would like to see in your life.
4. Ask a good friend for a list of the fruit observed in you and ask for brutal honesty *and* accept it.

Chapter 5

LOVE HAS NO OPPOSITE

There is no opposite of Love but it does have adversaries. In the Scripture, there are adversaries mentioned in relation to the lawlessness of those being opposed. In addition to these instances there were adversarial situations authorized for testing purposes. Thus the adversary's ultimate purpose is to test, train, and reveal the heart of the one being tested.

In Genesis 3, the adversary was the serpent. His job was to test Adam through Eve. Adam had walked in unity with Our Heavenly Father in the garden and had been given the task of naming all the animals. He was able to discern their character thus naming them according to their makeup. At that time Adam had both male and female characteristics within himself. However the hallmark aspect of Love is relationship and Our Heavenly Father saw that Adam should not be alone and would benefit from having a mate to share the wondrous creation hence Eve was brought forth.

I believe the couple walked in glorified bodies which provided a covering for them as they walked in unity with Our Heavenly Father for there had been no need for clothing to cover them up to this point. They were in communion with their Creator and had no restriction of intelligence or understanding. Adam had been placed in the garden and given the command: And the LORD God commanded the man, saying, of every tree of the garden thou mayest freely eat, But of the tree of the knowledge of good and evil, thou shalt not eat of it: for in the day that thou eatest thereof thou shalt surely die. (Genesis 2:16-17) What a simple command to keep but the choice was given to Adam: unity or lawlessness. I also believe this lasted 33 ½ years.

There are those who believe we have no choice but throughout Scripture we are shown that choices are given and choices are made. We do have free choice but with those choices come consequences. Free choice does not mean that there are no ramifications to those choices but it simply allows us to choose between two paths of growth and maturity: one in unity and one in adversity.

We are told that Eve was deceived but Adam wasn't. He decided to become lawless by eating of the fruit. Eve had already created her own interpretation of the Law by adding to it with the statement "neither shall ye touch it". It looks as though the first politician was found in Genesis. The Law could not be left alone but needed some fine tuning. Compromise which is an aspect of division and separation had already entered into the equation. All that was left was the physical act to complete the separation and exit from the garden. It was not until Adam partook of the fruit did the separation fully manifest. His communion with Our Heavenly Father was unplugged and the glory departed leaving him with nakedness and shame. This glory had departed and the unity of Love had been broken by the first Adam. This set the stage for the restoration of glory by the second Adam- Jesus Christ.

The adversary tested the hearts of Adam and Eve which began the thread of deception throughout Scripture. Deception is an aspect of lawlessness and is used by the ego to insure its control over the person who submits to it. Once Love reigns, deception is exposed by the light of truth and no longer has the insidious grip on the individual as it once did.

Division and separation are required for an adversary to successfully operate and prevail. In the United States, the society thrives on having some type of adversary whether it be an opposing football team, an inconsiderate driver, a selfish family member, or an irritating neighbor. Our ego would have us believe that we need an adversary to conquer, to blame, and to direct our focus. Why does our focus need redirecting? Our flesh wants to maintain control at all costs and knows that if we submit ourselves to the Love of Our Heavenly Father, the flesh will no longer rule and satisfy its lusts. Just as Eve added to the Law, our flesh has the need to rationalize why Our Heavenly

Father's Words need further interpretation or assistance in order to be fulfilled.

Division continued to grow on earth and the result was extreme lawlessness. Death began taking hold on the human body. The body was designed to live forever but without the glory produced from Love, it would begin to decay and death would infiltrate the genetics of the individuals. The longevity of individuals would diminish generation by generation. By the time Noah arrived on the scene, lawlessness had taken hold of the earth. Noah had bucked the trend and had not succumbed to the politically acceptable behavior of the day nor had his family. Don't you know that his contemporaries gave him a lot of grief about his lifestyle of righteousness?

Our Heavenly Father saw the condition of the earth, filled with lawlessness. Was it in His Power to rapture Noah and his family up to Heaven and simply wipe out the earth? Of course! Instead, He instructed Noah to build an ark which challenged all human reasoning. There was no ocean close by, there were no storm clouds on the horizon, and Noah had no apparent expertise as a shipbuilder. And to top it all off, it would take years to build not to mention the challenge of obtaining all the animals needed to populate it. However, Noah responded to the Word of THE LORD and eliminated the division that had prevailed. Once he selected unity over division, the project became a labor of Love that sustained him through the years it took to complete the ark.

As a type and shadow, Our Heavenly Father closed the door to the ark on the fateful day, Noah did not. Noah was not "raptured" from tribulation but was protected as it occurred. His lawfulness and desire to be in unity saved him from certain destruction. Our Heavenly Father initiated a covenant with Noah once the lawlessness was removed from the earth.

Jacob's life was full of deception, a fundamental flaw in his character. With the help of his mother, he attempted to gain his inheritance by deceiving Isaac into thinking he was Esau. Jacob and his mother Rebekah did not trust that Our Heavenly Father could bring forth Jacob's inheritance without a little help thus they resorted to

Ascending to Love

deception. Rather than act in Love and insure that Esau would receive the intended blessing, they took matters into their own hands and misrepresented Jacob to Isaac in his old age. This act created an adversary for Jacob and affected his decisions and success. Later on, Jacob would be deceived by his future father-in-law Laban and have to work twenty-one years for his wife instead of seven not to mention a second wife to care for in addition to the love of his life. Deception adds to complexity and the fruit creates unnecessary fear, uncertainty, doubt, strife, and contention. Only after Jacob had wrestled with the angel Peniel (the Face of GOD) did his deception finally surface in order to be dealt with. When he saw the Face of GOD, his character began to change. At the same time he would confront his adversary, Esau, only to find reconciliation rather than death.

In recent centuries, the church has given the adversary aka "the devil" undeserved power. Songs have been written about the battle in the heavenlies with Jesus and the devil punching it out in a boxing ring. The devil was poised to win the match but Our Heavenly Father showed up in the nick of time to push Jesus over the top. Come on, really? Who created the devil? The Creator of Heaven and earth! Who gave the devil power and authority? Our Heavenly Father! HIS perfect plan, will, and purpose will come forth and HE will send adversaries to those who attempt lawless acts against HIS ordained plan.

In the book of Numbers, chapter 22: Balak son of Zippor was king of the Moabites at this time. And he sent messengers to Balaam, son of Beor at Pethor, which is by the Euphrates River in the land of Amaw, to summon him, saying, "Look, a nation has come out of Egypt. They cover the face of the earth, and they are settling next to me. So now, please come and curse this nation.

In this passage there are a few things to consider. First, Balaam evidently had the power given by Our Heavenly Father to curse an entire nation. Impressive! Second, the children of Israel evoked fear into other nations simply from their presence because of the favor of Our Heavenly Father. Rather than pursue peace, their fear sought destruction. Our Heavenly Father spoke to Balaam and told him not to go to the Moabites. After declining their offer, the Moabites came back with a much better offer than before. Balaam entertained the deal which was a mistake. His ego was tweaked with a promise of wealth and recognition. Now it is time for the adversary to come on the scene and so Our Heavenly Father told him to travel to the Moabites' camp, a word opposite of the original Word given to Balaam by Our Heavenly Father.

> Num 22:22   And God's anger was kindled because he (Balaam) went: and the angel of the LORD stood in the way for an adversary (satan) against him. Now he was riding upon his ass, and his two servants [were] with him.

This story provides us with important insight to the judgment of disobedience. Our Heavenly Father gives us a directive to follow and we set it aside because of the idols in our heart. In this case it was fame and fortune for cursing the chosen nation of Our Heavenly Father. Once we compromise the directive, HE will answer us according to the idols of our heart and send an adversary to insure our failure. In the past, the church would have us believe that it is the powerful devil and that our path is acceptable thus never correcting the fundamental problem. People live their entire lives externalizing the adversary as a spiritual entity equivalent in power to Our Lord Jesus Christ and somehow omnipresent in order to wreak havoc among the saints around the world. In the meantime our ego keeps us bound up in illusions in order to control us and keep us from taking command and proceeding in Love. Are we being controlled by an illusion and fear?

Jesus provided us the blueprint for success over the "adversary". His ministry is being ordained and He has received His anointing and acceptance by Our Heavenly Father:

> Mat 3:16   And Jesus, when he was baptized, went up straightway out of the water: and, lo, the heavens were opened unto him, and he saw the Spirit of God descending like a dove, and lighting upon him:

Mat 3:17 And lo a voice from heaven, saying, This is my beloved Son, in whom I am well pleased.

Immediately upon receiving His marching orders, Jesus was led up of the Spirit into the wilderness to be tempted of the devil. What? Our Heavenly Father would send Jesus to be tempted of the devil? We tend to overlook the reality of the Word when it conflicts with repetitive preaching from an authoritative figure from a pulpit. The first thing that Jesus dealt with was the flesh. He spent forty days in a fast subjecting the flesh to hunger. Once the flesh was in extreme hunger, it was time for the adversary to take his best shot.

The first temptation was to have Jesus use His power of GOD particles (the smallest subatomic particle that retains its own identity) to turn stones into bread. The adversary tested Jesus in the area of submitting to his body's craving for food. After all, Jesus was completing a forty day fast. Jesus' responded, "It is written, Man shall not live by bread alone, but by every word that proceedeth out of the mouth of God."

The second temptation dealt with exercising authority: "If thou be the Son of God, cast thyself down: for it is written, He shall give his angels charge concerning thee: and in [their] hands they shall bear thee up, lest at any time thou dash thy foot against a stone." Once again the adversary knew that Jesus could command the angels to come to the rescue at a moments' notice. He responded again, "It is written again, Thou shalt not tempt the Lord thy God." Any authority exercised outside the Will of Our Heavenly Father is subject to judgment and its restitution.

The third and final temptation focused on exalting one's ego above Our Heavenly Father. "Again, the devil taketh him up into an exceeding high mountain, and sheweth him all the kingdoms of the world, and the glory of them; and saith unto him, All these things will I give thee, if thou wilt fall down and worship me." Adam had dominion and lost it when he chose separation from Our Heavenly Father. Jesus was to return that dominion through unity with Our Heavenly Father, not by exalting himself and perpetuating the division and separation. The adversary and the ego have the same agenda: control.

Personal assessment:
1. Do you have adversaries whose purpose in life is to make you miserable? Could this be due to your unwillingness to submit to a directive by Our Heavenly Father?
2. Have you attempted to minister life to any adversaries by blessing them with acts of Love?
3. If you have a weight problem, could it be due to your ego keeping a grip on your appetite in order to keep you in submission thus redirecting your focus away from spiritual matters?
4. Do you have fleshly cravings that preoccupy your thoughts and make you less productive?

Chapter 6
Love Your Enemies

The first use of Love in respect to being unconditional is in the 5th chapter of the Book of Matthew and included in what is known as "The Sermon on the Mount". Jesus had just begun His ministry after being tempted of the devil. He had been anointed by Our Heavenly Father and had spent forty days and nights in the wilderness being tempted. This event had been foretold by the Law of Sacrifice on the Day of Atonement in Leviticus 16. The High Priest was to sacrifice the first goat as a sin offering for the people. Its blood was sprinkled around the altar to atone of the uncleanness of the people. The High Priest would lay his hands on the head of the second goat and confess over it all the iniquities of the Israelites and all their transgressions in regard to all their sins. The High Priest would then send the goat away by the hand of a fit man into the wilderness. The "fit man" represents the Holy Ghost.

We commonly use the term "scapegoat" when someone is being sacrificed by the guilty as the offender or lawbreaker. The scapegoat is charged with the crime of others and suffers the consequences. The blameless goat became the focus of a legal proceeding in the Heavenly Court and was offered up for the sins of the people. The Heavenly statute in Leviticus conveyed the accountability of the sins to the goat. This statute of mercy provided a substitute for the necessary judgment of the Law and thus the acts of lawlessness were legally dealt with and there was no compromise allowing lawlessness to prevail.

This appearance in the Divine Court had to occur on an annual basis since the scapegoat was an animal and not a person. Not one person could be found innocent of sin allowing him or her to become the scapegoat and resolve the legal issue on a permanent basis. Year after year on the Day of Atonement, the High Priest would conduct the required ceremony to atone for the sins of himself and the people. The annual renewal of mercy was required because the Heavenly Court demanded a righteous verdict concerning the sins of the people.

This foreshadow places the baptism of Jesus on the Day of Atonement. He agreed to satisfy the full legal requirement to fulfill the righteousness of the Law, the character of Our Heavenly Father. It was a two part fulfillment with part one being at the beginning of His ministry and part two being at the Cross.

Jesus faced the chief enemy or adversary of Love immediately after being baptized. He fasted for forty days which brought his body into full submission of human frailty. By the fact that He was in the wilderness during the Feast of Tabernacles, it would imply that the Feast could not be fulfilled yet. While there was a time of celebration in Jerusalem, Jesus was in the wilderness preparing for a showdown with the chief adversary who had been operating with the legal right of dominion of the world. At the beginning of His ministry, Jesus was to obtain the legal right to challenge the current world authority. As the "second goat", he had the sins of the world on His head and had been led to the wilderness by the Holy Ghost in order that He could confront the chief enemy of Love. As mentioned earlier Jesus had to tested in all three core areas of testing. The first test had to occur at a high place, a metaphor of authority. Both understood power and authority better than anyone else walking the planet. They both understood all aspects of the Law as well as the physical laws. One was righteous called to fulfill the Law and the other's goal was to pervert the Law and its intent.

Do you think they simply walked up to some high mountain which at the time would take days to reach? Of course not. Their method transportation was no different than the angels showing up at a location in an instant. Both understood teleporting between two places. Additionally, Jesus did not challenge the devil's legal claim over the kingdoms of the world and his ability to assign legal title to Jesus. Jesus knew that his next forty-two months were going to culminate in his death at the Cross and he could not circumvent one aspect of the mission of regaining title over all mankind. Furthermore, the overall mission required a uncompromised righteous outcome. Satan understood what was at stake if Jesus fulfilled His earthly calling. Once again, Jesus replied with the Word of GOD. "Away with you, Satan! For it is written, 'You shall worship the LORD your God, and Him only you shall serve.'"

Love responds righteously to all enemies.

> Matthew 5:43 "You have heard that it was said, 'You shall love your neighbor and hate your enemy.'
> 44 But I say to you, love your enemies, bless those who curse you, do good to those who hate you, and pray for those who spitefully use you and persecute you,
> 45 that you may be sons of your Father in heaven; for He makes His sun rise on the evil and on the good, and sends rain on the just and on the unjust.
> 46 For if you love those who love you, what reward have you? Do not even the tax collectors do the same?

In the New Testament, the first use of "agape" was contained in the Sermon on the Mount. Jesus dispelled the notion of division by commanding us to not only love our neighbors but love our enemies as well. Once He spoke this, the revelation of unity was given to all mankind and the ramifications of this revelation are far reaching. If we are to love our neighbor and our enemy, who else is there? Nobody! Are Christians to love Muslims, Hindus, Agnostics, and Atheists? Yes to all of the above.

Man's ego seeks division because division breeds control. Men want to control other men thus they create structure placing them above other men. Most church denominations have followed this path by creating a structure that perpetuates control over the congregation. You only need to look as far as church history to find such a theme. Over the centuries, the Catholic Church controlled the masses by restricting access to the Scriptures from the common man so that the clergy had exclusive use of existing Bibles. The masses were convinced that the clergy's revelation of Scriptures were accurate and they were required to comply with the structure, rules and regulations set forth by the Pope whether they agreed with the true Word of GOD or not. At various and sundry points in time, parishioners were able to pay for removal of sins, a very lucrative procedure established by those in control. The church dissuaded the common man from seeking a personal relationship with Our Heavenly Father and that the only access had to be through the church hierarchy.

Jesus promoted unity among mankind and Our Heavenly Father. He promoted individual prayer to our Heavenly Father and seeking the Holy Spirit's counsel in all matters. How can we fully hear Our Heavenly Father if we have an issue with an enemy that redirects our focus toward revenge? An adversary's subtle task is to move our time and resources away from our calling and redirected to the adversity at hand. This can take place over days, months, or even years. Our growth requires obstacles but we are not to let those obstacles keep us from fulfilling the very reason we are placed on this earth- to Love and to teach Love.

One of the greatest and true tests of our heart is if we can love our enemies. This is a commandment of Jesus to all mankind. When you can truly say that you love your enemy, you will then know that you have unconditional love in your heart. Does this mean you must endorse their behavior? No. It means that you must carry no malice towards them and you should seek to understand them and what motivates their actions. Is there something you could do to minister to them that might effect a positive relationship towards you? Seeking the counsel of the Most Holy Spirit will help you move towards reconciliation versus further division. Love unites, not divides.

One day, one of the greatest enemies of Jesus to walk the earth was walking down the road to Damascus. This man had never met Jesus during His forty-two month ministry yet the man was zealous after the traditions of his fathers to eliminate all those who continued to carry forth the message of Jesus after His death. He believed his purpose in life was to extinguish the Gospel of Jesus Christ. Is there a greater adversary than this? His resumé reads as follows:

Circumcised the eighth day, of the stock of Israel, [of] the tribe of Benjamin, an Hebrew of the Hebrews; as touching the law, a Pharisee; concerning zeal, persecuting the church; touching the righteousness which is in the law, blameless. (Philippians 3:5-6 KJV)

He was well educated, accepted by the church, passionate about his vocation, and held in high esteem by his peers. He had the full package. However, extinguishing the Gospel was not his calling. Just the opposite- to spread the Gospel to the uttermost parts of the earth, to the Gentiles whom he called foreigners. His name was Saul.

Jesus was not moved by Saul's zeal and intent. Being the chief enemy of the Gospel, Saul needed a close encounter with Our Lord Jesus Christ. Jesus needed to appear to Saul in a physical manifestation and chose the road to Damascus as the meeting place. Saul was not seeking a relationship in any manner whatsoever. However, Saul had a calling on his life that Love required to be fulfilled. He was a chosen vessel for the spreading of the Gospel. He was called to that task before entering the womb. Love would not be denied. Saul's stubbornness necessitated extreme measures including a Divine encounter with subsequent blindness to bring home the point. Saul's name means "desire". I would suggest that "strong desire and will of the ego" best described Saul. Saul's gifts were in operation but perversity had surrounded his calling. I'm sure his parents developed and trained him according to his natural inclinations toward education and The Law. As parents, we should look for those talents of our children and further develop them. Saul had fully embraced his gifts.

Saul's calling had been perverted by the belief of entitlement that was pervasive in the church. The Jews looked at all foreigners as second class citizens. How could Saul be caught teaching them? Love had a different idea. When confronted by Jesus after His resurrection, Saul now had irrefutable evidence contrary to the beliefs ingrained in him by the church. Furthermore, the physical blindness was the second witness to this encounter. One day he was at the top of his game, the next day his job is gone and he is blind. His ego must have been spinning.

Once Love arrived, perversity departed and the man was humbled. His name had to be changed to an appropriate one. "Paul" which is Latin for "small or little" was appropriate. It was as though the name change reflected the change in the ego from one of strong desire and domination to small or little. Perfect! Now this vessel of honor is ready to embrace the calling. He would go on to write fifteen Epistles in the New Testament. The fifteenth is the Book of Hebrews which is mathematically proven to be consistent with Paul's other writings thus I agree with his authorship.

What lessons can we learn from the conversion of Saul? First, if you are convinced your doctrine is solid and cannot be challenged, think again. Your core assumptions can be totally wrong even though the church's teaching may not have previously been challenged. Secondly, adversity or blindness may play a part in your conversion to the Truth thus adversity should be embraced rather than avoided. Thirdly, you may be an adversary of the true Gospel and your traditions and ego have been your greatest obstacle to the true revelation of Love. Fourthly, your adversary may be Our Heavenly Father in disguise. Each and every person born on this earth was created and ordained by Our Heavenly Father with the core intent of Love. As we move closer to Our Heavenly Father, we will come to understand this truth. When we actually see the Face of GOD in our enemies, we will truly grasp the revelation of loving our enemies. The end result is restoration.

Personal Assessment:
1. Make a list of "enemies".
2. Make a list of steps that promote restoration.
3. Take action to convert those enemies to friends.
4. How are you accountable for making or promoting the other person's alienation towards you?
5. How do you think Jesus would convert the enemy?

Chapter 7

The Consummation of Love

The word "perfection" implies an absolute state without the slightest flaw thus when we hear this term and attempt to apply it to ourselves we often give up before we even pursue it. Our minds tell us that since we cannot achieve "perfection", why try? Let us discuss perfect Love as John wrote the following:

1 John 4:17 Love has been perfected (teleioō) among us in this: that we may have boldness in the day of judgment; because as He is, so are we in this world. 18 There is no fear in love; but perfect love casts out fear, because fear involves torment. But he who fears has not been made perfect in love. 19 We love Him because He first loved us.

Teleioō (perfected) is defined as follows:
1) to make perfect, complete
a) to carry through completely, to accomplish, finish, bring to an end
2) to complete (perfect)
a) add what is yet wanting in order to render a thing full
b) to be found perfect
3) to bring to the end (goal) proposed
4) to accomplish
a) bring to a close or fulfilment by event
1) of the prophecies of the scriptures

Jesus came forth as Love to show us what perfect Love is. He reconciled the world to Our Heavenly Father and provided us a means to attain perfect Love, He is our example. We often relate with others in the Bible such as David, Daniel, and Joseph but we should focus our attention on Jesus Christ, HIS Beloved Son. Our minds would convince us that becoming like Jesus "The Perfect" is unattainable. However, John tells us in this passage "as He is, so are we in this world" thus we can be perfect as well. As we pursue the Love walk, we will be transformed into perfect Love. Just as we were baptized in The Holy Spirit, we can be baptized in Love. We can be so immersed in His Love that we will experience a transformation in our lives. Of this I am convinced.

There is no fear in Love, perfect Love actually casts out fear. Did Jesus fear? There is absolutely no record of Him fearing anything. He knew Our Heavenly Father would accomplish HIS perfect plan, will, and purpose for HIS Son. Jesus dealt with the same realities and temptations we all deal with in that He made Himself of no reputation, taking the form of a bondservant, and coming in the likeness of men. Our egos would have us believe there is an adversary that must be dealt with who is able to overcome us and subdue us into slavery thus fear is created and maintained by having this adversary. Fear, if given authority, has the ability to enslave, isolate, destroy, change our physiology, lose our focus, forget our calling, and totally incapacitate us to the point of worthlessness.

How often are we told in Scripture to "fear not"? Are you in fear of something? When we become scarcity oriented, we set ourselves up to be fear motivated. As we simplify our lives, we find that we need less to live on and move away from hoarding, a fear-based attitude. As we pursue a Love relationship with Our Heavenly Father, fear dissipates. The closer we move to Our Heavenly Father the more we are motivated by Love. Our intent is Love based not fear based. We have an assurance and peace that is perfected by Love in order that we may have boldness in the day of judgment. What is this boldness? It is the confidence that we attained this mature Love walk and acted accordingly, not by fear of being thrown into an everlasting hell, but by the desire to become one with Our Heavenly Father.

Fear causes torment and destruction. Ulcers are a common occurrence of those who are consumed with fear. They may have

Ascending to Love

grown up in a household based in fear and rejection. They may have been abused by a loved one which planted a seed of inadequacy and shame. A teacher may have spoken a curse over them and convinced them that they could never achieve success. Fear is used to control and enslave by those in authority to insure their position of power over those who will submit to such conditions. Populations are controlled by such means. The threat of destruction, incarceration, loss of wealth, all play an important role by those in power over nations to keep the population from rising up against them in rebellion.

As Jesus is, so are we in this world. We are given an assurance that we can walk as Jesus walked. He was subjected to temptation just as we are. He was given the opportunity to "control" and walk by His ego. Instead, He commanded rather than controlled. Command comes by authority whereas control comes by manipulation and lawlessness. Within in it, Love has lawful power to command the particles of the universe. Throughout Scripture Love superseded the natural laws. How was Jesus able to change the water into wine? By Love. He commanded the GOD particles to take on the attributes of wine rather than water. How was He able to multiply the bread and the fishes? By Love. Once again, He commanded the particles to magnetically attract at the quantum level and order themselves as bread and fishes.

But wait! Jesus did all these things before He went to the Cross! He was not operating in a glorified body! Calvary had not yet occurred. What was the key to His ability to command the particles, walk on water, become invisible, operate in all the gifts of the Spirit? Love! The character of Our Heavenly Father provides an inherent source of power over the creation that was derived from HIS character. The intent of Love created this ever-expanding universe. Yes, the big bang occurred but an explosion/expansion is preceded by a compression. A compression is preceded by intent and the intent was Love. Therefore, Love created the universe and everything in it. The universe will respond to Love because each particle will submit to the character of the Creator. We can now begin to understand the verse:

John 14:12 "Most assuredly, I say to you, he who believes in Me, the works that I do he will do also; and greater works than these he will do, because I go to My Father."

Jesus legally brought life and the fullness of Love to each and every one of us. He became our example of how to walk in this body that Our Heavenly Father ordained we walk in. Would He make such a bold statement of "greater works" if we did not have the ability to fulfill those words of boldness? What keeps us from that fulfillment? The flesh would want us to focus on any other topic than Love. Hope focuses on the future and there is nothing wrong in considering the future. Faith is the substance of things hoped for and the evidence of things not seen. Love is now and the manifestation of Love is seen, touched, and perceived with the eye. The multitudes ate the fishes and bread until their hunger was satisfied. The abundance beyond the need was sufficient for the boy who brought the "down payment" to be amply compensated for his willingness to share the loaves and fishes. Love is generous.

Why do we steer away from the "greater works" statement? Our ego would have us believe that we cannot operate in similar fashion because of the sin in our life. It stirs up memories of misconduct, lawlessness, lust of the flesh, pride, and lust of the eyes. In different parts of the world, sin is rampant and many of us are exposed to it on a daily basis. Our ego would have us believe that walking in greater works is out of our grasp and we should not even attempt or pursue it because we will surely fail. Our failure will then bring guilt and rejection. However, Love forgives, Love reconciles, Love thinks no uncomely thought, and Love most of all restores. If we fall, Love picks us up. If we are guilty, Love restores and reconciles us. If we are fearful, Love will cast out our fear and restore peace.

Are you being tormented? Torment is caused by fear. Pursue Love and fear WILL depart and with it torment becomes a thing of the past. The past no longer exists even though there are some people who spend their life in the past. Once again, their ego controls them by keeping their focus in the past whether it be guilt oriented or pride oriented. Those who have attended high school class reunions have probably observed former classmates who still live in the past. The football hero or homecoming queen may try to relive the past since the present is not as glamorous or successful. If they were to focus on Love, new memories would outshine the old ones. There are opportunities every single day to express Love and change lives. Love will seek out opportunities to cover the earth with its character. Love does not promote fear and torment but causes it to dissipate in its very presence. Love will discern the answer to the problem plaguing a person who is in fear of loss. Wisdom is summoned by Love along with understanding to focus on an answer that has been just beyond the reach of the individual who has been placed in your path. It is your eyes of understanding that can pierce the veil of blindness. Love will attract those who need your counsel. Though you never saw yourself as a counselor, Love will thrust you into this role to prevent the dire consequences of torment, fear, rejection, and even loss of life.

How do we know when we are mature in Love? Count the number of enemies you have. Are there zero? Who are your adversaries? Who do you avoid at all costs? Do you want to sue anybody today? What are you afraid of? Who do you hate? When was the last time your heart was gripped with fear? "He that feareth is not made perfect in love."

> 1 John 4:20 If a man says, I love God, and hateth his brother, he is a liar: for he that loveth not his brother whom he hath seen, how can he love God whom he hath not seen?

By honestly asking yourself these questions, you can assess your current state. Don't be discouraged if you do have enemies and adversaries, fear and torment. We all have to start somewhere. The key is to move forward and mature in Love. Do not let your current state define your future. The future is subject to your decision to change and pursue a life immersed in Love. My focus on the revelation of Love began in the year 2005. That does not mean that I did not operate in Love in the past. I used the Love chapter of 1 Corinthians 13 to propose to my wife of 39 years. My understanding of that Scripture was no different than the understanding of addition and subtraction in the field of mathematics to a ten year old. That aspect of math is needed before the student could tackle algebra, geometry, and calculus. We build on our foundation of knowledge, skill, wisdom, and understanding. You are reading this book because deep down you know there is a greater revelation of Love to be obtained. All of creation groans for the fullness of times. The fullness of times will be ushered in by the revelation of Love for Love IS the character of Our Creator who is also Our Heavenly Father. As we become immersed in Love, greater works will manifest and the fulfillment of those words of Jesus will be at hand.

Personal Assessment:
1. Do you see yourself currently moving toward Love or away from Love?
2. What hinders you from being a greater expression of Love?
3. What actions in the last week testify of being Love to others?
4. What actions last week were an indictment of your lack of Love?

Chapter 8
THE ELEVENTH COMMANDMENT

As Jesus told His disciples, He came not to do away with the Law but to fulfill the Law. Members of his staff of twelve were raised from children on the Levitical Law. Everyone was aware of the Ten Commandments and I am sure most were acquainted with the 613 commandments and statutes contained in the Books of the Law.

Jesus knew that His hour was at hand when He would go to the Cross and redeem all of mankind. He was in the midst of having His last meal with the disciples and took time to wash their feet, a task of a servant. Here we have the Son of the Lord God Almighty washing feet and you can be assured that those feet needed washing. Jesus needed to bring forth a truth in a manner that all could understand, the concept of unconditional Love agapaō.

"He loved them to the end" was an unfailing, unconditional Love that even included loving the one who would betray you. Jesus washed Judas Iscariot's feet as well. He knew that Judas was the one who would be used to facilitate the trip to the Cross. Judas was the treasurer and once again money provided the catalyst to bring forth evil. One should think twice about wanting to be a treasurer for the Kingdom. The love of money or "greed" is the root of all evil. If one does not have a heart for charity, the entanglements of greed can with great subtlety overpower the weak.

Peter in his usual "act first think later" fashion did not understand what Jesus was teaching with the washing of the feet. Peter disagreed with the ceremony and failed to see the big picture. Isn't that like us to immediately challenge what we don't understand when if we wait and keep silent, the Spirit of GOD would minister the truth and revelation about the event? Peter's impetuous traits prior to receiving the baptism of the Holy Spirit and power from on High provided us with optimism that we can change as well. Once Our Lord Jesus Christ explained the foot washing to Peter, the pendulum swung to the other extreme. Wash everything!

Jesus gave the disciples an example of service to others. To appreciate what was being said, the Jews were placed under subjection to Rome. They were looking for a conquering messiah to overtake their enemies and place them back in control. When Jesus arrived on the scene, the masses failed to recognize Him. They had been taught to believe a paradigm that kept them from recognizing the Son of GOD in the flesh! Their blindness had caused them to miss a blessing. How often are the traditions of man to blame for the lack of fruitfulness in one's life.

It is easy to love your friends but what about your enemies? With the knowledge that Judas would betray Him, Jesus washed his feet. How many of us can say we would do the same with the purest of intent? What was Judas thinking as his feet were being washed? Was regret beginning to set in? Was there a core craving that could not be overcome? Greed (or fear of scarcity) was at the root of this craving. It has been reported that Judas was from an influential family and was accustomed to having money. Among the twelve disciples, Judas had been the clear choice to be the treasurer. There is no record of any of the disciples disputing the calling of Judas. Just as Judah had betrayed Joseph by selling him to the Ishmeelites, Judas did the same to Jesus and sold Him to the chief priests.

The Ishmeelites were descendants of Ishmael. Ishmael laid claim to the wealth of Abraham, being the first son but he was not the son of promise. There was no love between the Jews and Ishmeelites. It is only appropriate that Joseph's future would be placed in the hands of the descendents who felt they should have the inheritance that would ultimately be conveyed to Joseph. The trials and tests of Joseph provide us with assurance that in spite of our enemies, our calling will prevail. Joseph served his "enemies" for 13 years. He was despitefully accused and thrown in prison but the prison could not keep him from ascending into his calling. By the time he had completed his 13 year training period, he was well equipped to manage the global assets of Egypt.

So often we focus on self serving examples to pattern our life after. Often it is a character from a movie or television series. These larger than life actors present an illusion of success and prosperity that would have us believe their lie. On the other hand, we might take an isolated act of Jesus or another example in the Bible and base our response on a Scripture taken out of context. Why don't we focus on the specific words of Jesus:

> John 13:15 For I have given you an example, that ye should do as I have done to you. (KJV)

He gave His disciples (and us) a specific example to live by- serve others even if your enemy is among them. Your enemy will ultimately be reconciled to Our Heavenly Father and thus become your brother. As you walk in Love with your enemy, you set the stage for his conviction of sin. In the Heavenly Court, his actions are judged to be unlawful as compared to yours. Your response of Love enables the High Court to rule in your favor. By responding to our enemies in like fashion to their acts, we usurp the Court's right to rule on our behalf. Our Heavenly Father is capable of righteously judging our enemies without our intervention.

The feet symbolize our walk or our calling. It is where the "rubber" meets the road. Is our walk leading us to death and destruction or life and fruitfulness? Clean feet were required to stand on Holy Ground. You were required to remove your shoes. Dust and sweat represent the curse placed on Adam. The disciples needed to be cleansed of the curse. This could only be accomplished by Love. Jesus provided a clear example of loving your brother. His earthly ministry was coming to an end. He had healed the sick, preached the Good News to the masses, and set the captives free. His disciples had been trained for nearly 42 months and now needed the key to continue the ministry- Love.

The disciples had to understand that this Love Jesus was talking about was not the conditional love they were accustomed to and experienced from an early age. His acts were intended to ingrain into their understanding the unconditional Love even towards their enemies. Jesus wrapped a towel, or apron, around Himself while washing the feet of those He chose to spread the Gospel. The apron symbolizes service to others. Here we have the Son of GOD wearing an apron. How often have we projected an attitude of arrogance toward a waiter? Who are we to place ourselves above Our Lord Jesus Christ who felt it was not beneath Him to wear an apron and wash the dirt and grime from men's feet? No one would argue that if the wealthiest man on earth would promote such an act of service that those of lesser means should do the same!

Jesus spoke "For I have given you an example, that ye should do as I have done to you." He is preparing the disciples for the Eleventh Commandment. As always, He gave them a great example to remember, to be burned into their consciousness. There would never be a question of interpretation by the recipients of this great Commandment. No theological scholars could spend hours in the Temple debating its meaning or intent. This commandment could not be converted to some watered down custom and lose the power of its message. "If I then, your Lord and Master, have washed your feet; ye also ought to wash one another's feet." The die is cast! Service to others, even the most menial task, is the mandate of the Kingdom.

"Verily, verily, I say unto you, The servant is not greater than his lord; neither he that is sent greater than he that sent him." Listen up! None of you can claim exemption from this Commandment, in modern terms. This Commandment comes directly from the Throne Room of Our Heavenly Father. Would Our Heavenly Father wash our feet? Certainly! Every Commandment reveals HIS character!

You will be blessed if you do these things! As you serve others with a servant's heart, the blessings of service will overtake you. Remember, it is a heart issue. Judas Iscariot was still in the room as Jesus was speaking these things. Judas' focus was on the money, not the service to mankind. Judas knew Jesus could overcome those in

Ascending to Love

charge with another miracle. He could then take the money given to him by the church officials and place it in the treasury and would be a hero among the disciples. His plot was flawed but Jesus knew that the pride and ego would be unable to thwart the Plan of Salvation. The path to the Cross requires death to the ego and what better irony than to have man's ego send itself to death!

Judas departed before Jesus enacted the Eleventh Commandment. This Commandment was withheld until Judas left to fulfill his calling. This calling was necessary to complete the requirement for salvation to be presented to all mankind. In his own way, Judas was a necessary piece to the puzzle. Evil entered into Judas by name "Adversary or Devil". The adversary would be in conflict with this Eleventh Commandment. The pride and ego of man would never conform to the Eleventh Commandment. "I'm too good to serve the peons." "Look at all the schooling I've completed." "Look at my achievements, I must be special." Pride and ego will create thousands of reasons not to serve those of lesser means. Had Judas fully complied with the Eleventh Commandment, he would not have betrayed his Master. Love would have prevented evil from entering in. The plan was to be fulfilled right on time and in proper order.

The Eleventh Commandment: A new commandment I give unto you, That ye love one another; as I have loved you, that ye also love one another.

Personal Assessment:
1. What sacrifice of Love did you make for another person this week?
2. Did anyone make a sacrifice of Love for you recently?
3. If so, did you express your gratitude for that act?
4. Did you initiate an act of Love toward an enemy this week?
5. Have you expressed your Love for Our Heavenly Father lately?

Chapter 9
THE JUDGMENT OF LOVE

The Ten Commandments were designed to establish and standard of conduct, maintain order among the people, and reveal the character of Our Heavenly Father. Ultimately, they are the commandments of Love. The bringing forth of the Law exposed sin, lawlessness, and evil. We have all broken the law at some point but the question is this, are we habitual lawbreakers? Our Heavenly Father's grace and mercy are designed to restore and reconcile us from sin and lawlessness. But ultimately habitual sin has a judgment that demands payment. Love will evoke a judgment of correction and restoration that may be painful to the emotions or the physical body. If our body is our "Temple", why do we violate it so much with toxins? Our cravings, if left unrestrained, will abuse our physical bodies to the point of death. No drug addict started out to be a perpetual abuser.

The 613 commandments and statutes mentioned in the Old Testament addressed many needed judgments for the children of Israel who lived before the arrival of Jesus, the perfect sacrifice. Many sacrifices of substitute animals were used to provide forgiveness of sin on a temporary basis. Year after year the symbolic sacrifices were made in preparation of the supreme sacrifice of Love. Until this hallmark of Love presented itself, the revelation of Love as reflected in the Law could not be comprehended by the people. Until then, the Israelites had a difficult time obeying the Law and thus brought on the judgments of the Law. These judgments focused on the physical even though they were spiritual in origin.

When the casual reader proceeds through the Old Testament, there is a lack of understanding of the judgments of the Law. He or she sees Our Heavenly Father as a mean and vindictive Creator, a taskmaster at best. Nothing could be further from the truth. The assumption is that physical death is the ultimate punishment, a soul-centric view. From the spiritual perspective of eternal life and ultimate redemption by a loving Heavenly Father, physical death is a release from the sin nature until the perfect plan of salvation has been consummated, the true act of Love. As we read through the Book of Judges, we find that Our Heavenly Father sends a solution each and every time the Israelites get into a mess only to see them return to their wicked ways again and again. When we move from a soul-centric point of view to a spirit-centered basis of understanding, we are able to see the unfolding plan of redemption in the various books of the Old Testament. Our physical life is only a small aspect of our infinite existence with Our Heavenly Father and a judgment resulting in physical death can then be seen as an act of mercy rather than a response of rage by an angry god.

Most of us have been conditioned to assume Love to be a passive, non-confrontational state of emotions that cower under pressure. Nothing could be further from the truth. Unconditional Love is active and overcomes all obstacles, lawlessness, and acts of aggression. Love begins with grace and mercy to allow the recipient the opportunity to repent or change direction from the path of destruction. Patience and longsuffering allow the sinner time for a heart change to take place. Warnings are issued so that the lawbreaker can come to the realization that his actions will have undesired consequences. However at some point of discernment from the Holy Spirit, active judgment initiates a response. The judgment will fit the law being broken. Our Heavenly Father will "repay" the sinner with righteous judgment in accordance to the Law being broken.

Jesus provides us the perfect example of the Lawgiver. The Gospels provide us an excellent perspective of Our Heavenly Father's character which is reflected in His Son. "I and My Father are One" is a clear statement of fact and truth. In His earthly ministry, Jesus displayed both compassion and judgment. He raised the dead, forgave the sinner, displayed compassion to the multitudes, healed the sick, fed the hungry, and enlightened the misguided. But as needed, He evoked judgment. We know that greed is the root of all evil. In Matthew 21, Jesus cleansed the Temple of greed:

> 12 And Jesus went into the temple of God, and cast out all them that sold and bought in the temple, and overthrew the tables of the moneychangers, and the seats of them that sold doves,
> 13 And said unto them, It is written, My house shall be called the house of prayer; but ye have made it a den of thieves.
> 14 And the blind and the lame came to him in the temple; and he healed them. (NKJV)

It would seem that the natural odds were against Him. There was more than one moneychanger and we would expect them to be irritated with someone attacking their business. They had rationalized in their hearts the need to place their business at the source of demand- The Temple. Each Israelite was to give a half shekel according to the statute in Exodus 30 for the service of the Temple. The moneychangers would make change for a profit. The people also needed doves for sacrifice and where better to get the doves than right there at the table of the moneychanger. How efficient!

Upon cleansing the Temple, Jesus makes a statement, "My house shall be called the house of prayer; but ye have made it a den of thieves". Greed had replace communion with Our Heavenly Father in the Temple. No wonder we are told that greed is the root of all evil. Greed assumes scarcity and convinces us that we must obtain money by any means necessary to assure our future. Communion with Our Heavenly Father proves that assumption to be false. HE provides for all our need according to His Riches.

Jesus cleansed the Temple a second time in Mark 11:

> 15 And they come to Jerusalem: and Jesus went into the temple, and began to cast out them that sold and bought in the temple, and overthrew the tables of the moneychangers,

Ascending to Love

and the seats of them that sold doves;
16 And would not suffer that any man should carry [any] vessel through the temple.
17 And he taught, saying unto them, Is it not written, My house shall be called of all nations the house of prayer? but ye have made it a den of thieves.

This time we see there were additional merchants in the Temple. Was this the precursor to a shopping mall? He further expanded the description of the Temple when He used the term "of all nations". So now we have two witnesses in Scripture establishing the importance of cleansing greed from the Temple. The ramifications of these two acts are dramatic. Love will not tolerate habitual greed to thrive, especially in the place of Communion with Our Heavenly Father. At a personal level, as we pursue greed we evoke a judgment upon us and our personal temple must also get cleansed of the unrighteousness.

Greed is subtle, dangerous, sinister, and menacing. Get the picture? A Christian's ego will rationalize the greed by proclaiming the unrighteous accumulation of wealth to be a blessing and an answer to prayer. This is the subtle aspect of greed. Can greed be a result of prayer? Yes. A very specific Scripture in Ezekiel 14 reveals this truth:

1 Then came certain of the elders of Israel unto me, and sat before me.
2 And the word of the LORD came unto me, saying,
3 Son of man, these men have set up their idols in their heart, and put the stumblingblock of their iniquity before their face: should I be enquired of at all by them?
4 Therefore speak unto them, and say unto them, Thus saith the Lord GOD; Every man of the house of Israel that setteth up his idols in his heart, and putteth the stumblingblock of his iniquity before his face, and cometh to the prophet; I the LORD will answer him that cometh according to the multitude of his idols;

5 That I may take the house of Israel in their own heart, because they are all estranged from me through their idols.
6 Therefore say unto the house of Israel, Thus saith the Lord GOD; Repent, and turn [yourselves] from your idols; and turn away your faces from all your abominations.

    This passage is very important to our understanding of the ego and the sinister side of its willingness to deceive us and separate us from Love. These certain elders were men of experience, not young and immature. Ezekiel discerned their hearts and perceived there to be idols that were blinding them. He called these idols "stumblingblocks of their iniquity" asked Our Heavenly Father if he should even give them an audience. Our Heavenly Father's response is very illuminating to our understanding. Yes, give each man an audience and I the LORD will answer him that cometh according to the multitude of his idols. The response to your prayer for wealth and riches can be answered by Our Heavenly Father according to the idols in your heart. You hear HIS voice and respond. The manifestation of the apparent blessings will end in judgment and you will wonder why. You only have to look as far as your heart to find the answer. The subtle deceit in your heart must be exposed. Your idols have estranged you from an intimate relationship with Our Heavenly Father.

    How dangerous are those idols in the heart! This is why we MUST focus on Love and its cleansing attributes. As we immerse ourselves in Love, the idols will be removed and the ego and its controlling motives are replaced by Love and its commands. Our Heavenly Father promises us blessing, fruitfulness, and increase but it must be the result of our Love walk, not the exploitation of others. The judgment of Love will expose greed and all its subtleties. This is the corrective and cleansing aspect of Love. If we are called to judge the nations, our hearts must be purified by the cleansing fire of Love. How can we be entrusted with much wealth if there lies a subtle idol within the recesses of our heart? Our temple must be cleansed.

Ascending to Love

The ultimate goal of judgment is restoration of the Love walk. None of us want to be called strangers by Our Heavenly Father. We do not want to be told, "Depart from me" as in Matthew 7:

> 17 Even so every good tree bringeth forth good fruit; but a corrupt tree bringeth forth evil fruit.
> 18 A good tree cannot bring forth evil fruit, neither [can] a corrupt tree bring forth good fruit.
> 19 Every tree that bringeth not forth good fruit is hewn down, and cast into the fire.
> 20 Wherefore by their fruits ye shall know them.
> 21 Not every one that saith unto me, Lord, Lord, shall enter into the kingdom of heaven; but he that doeth the will of my Father which is in heaven.
> 22 Many will say to me in that day, Lord, Lord, have we not prophesied in thy name? and in thy name have cast out devils? and in thy name done many wonderful works?
> 23 And then will I profess unto them, I never knew you: depart from me, ye that work iniquity. (KJV)

The above Scripture confirms the Ezekiel passage. Jesus did not question their works. They did prophesy, cast out devils, and did many wonderful works but their motives were not of Love. Jesus classified them as strangers and workers of iniquity. Selfish motivations can and will produce apparent spiritual-based results for the Word of GOD has the power within itself to cause itself to come to pass. The Word has the force of life and creativity in it. The universe is still expanding because of the Word. However, if you use the Word of GOD with the wrong intent, the judgment of Love will prevail and you will go through the fire cleansing process to remove the leaven from your heart. The more leaven found, the more intense the heat. You will see the confrontational facet of Love in action and it will be painful to your flesh. The purging process is never an enjoyable experience. This is why Jesus made it perfectly clear that Love is the Way. Love is the Key of David. If you want to be lawful, you must pursue the revelation of Love. With this understanding, we can better understand the words of Jesus in Matthew 22:

> 36 Master, which [is] the great commandment in the law?
> 37 Jesus said unto him, Thou shalt love the Lord thy God with all thy heart, and with all thy soul, and with all thy mind.
> 38 This is the first and great commandment.
> 39 And the second [is] like unto it, Thou shalt love thy neighbour as thyself.
> 40 On these two commandments hang all the law and the prophets. (KJV)

The Law and the Prophets are summed up by Love. In Luke 10, Jesus emphasizes "all":

> 27 And he answering said, Thou shalt love the Lord thy God with all thy heart, and with all thy soul, and with all thy strength, and with all thy mind; and thy neighbour as thyself.

Each and every word spoken by Jesus was motivated by Love. Words of judgment had their basis of Love. When Jesus said "depart", this was not for an eternity but lawlessness must not stand before Love as though it has been sanctioned and endorsed. Correction and cleansing must occur before those men could dwell with Our Heavenly Father.

Paul, formerly Saul, is credited for writing two thirds of the books in the New Testament. After Jesus, we would expect Paul to have great understanding about the Kingdom of GOD and how it operates. He is introduced in Acts 7:58 as the official over the stoning of Stephen. He was an expert on the Mosaic Law which had become tradition and had no understanding of the intent of Love behind the Law. His purpose in life was to persecute Christians who appeared to be breaking the Law. He was an adversary or "satan" to the Christians. Paul gave his approval to stone Stephen to death for his belief in Jesus Christ as the Son of the Most High God:

Ascending to Love

Act 7:58 And cast [him] out of the city, and stoned [him]: and the witnesses laid down their clothes at a young man's feet, whose name was Saul.
59 And they stoned Stephen, calling upon [God], and saying, Lord Jesus, receive my spirit.
60 And he kneeled down, and cried with a loud voice, Lord, lay not this sin to their charge. And when he had said this, he fell asleep. (KJV)

The blood of Stephen was on Saul's hands. However, Stephen spoke mercy over Saul when he said, "Lord, lay not this sin to their charge". This prayer laid the groundwork for Love to judge Saul with mercy rather than the judgment of death.

Saul was zealous in his efforts to carry out the persecutions. He was wreaking havoc in the church and put many Christians in prison. There was no greater adversary than Saul. "And Saul, yet breathing out threatenings and slaughter against the disciples of the Lord, went unto the high priest." Then something happened to Saul in Acts 9:

3 As he journeyed he came near Damascus, and suddenly a light shone around him from heaven.
4 Then he fell to the ground, and heard a voice saying to him, "Saul, Saul, why are you persecuting Me?"
5 And he said, "Who are You, Lord?"
Then the Lord said, "I am Jesus, whom you are persecuting. It is hard for you to kick against the goads."
6 So he, trembling and astonished, said, "Lord, what do You want me to do?"
Then the Lord said to him, "Arise and go into the city, and you will be told what you must do."

Saul met Love face to face but the men who journeyed with him stood speechless, hearing a voice, but seeing no man. Saul was now blind and they led him by the hand and brought him into Damascus.

He was three days without sight, and neither ate nor drank. Saul's true calling was about to begin after a life of being an adversary to Love. His GOD given gifts enabled him to persecute the Christians rather than serve them. The gifts without the right motivation will cause death and destruction. Saul's blindness was both physical and spiritual.

Now we are introduced to another man: Ananias whose name means "whom Jehovah has graciously given". For three days Saul had been praying. I'm sure he had included the restoration of sight to his prayer. His prayer to have his eyes opened both spiritually and physically were met with a vision from Above. The vision revealed to Saul that Ananias was coming to heal him. Jesus called Ananias "to go to Saul" and minister healing to him. He was not excited about the request to go to the enemy of the Christians. Gulp!

But the Lord said to him, "Go, for he is a chosen vessel of Mine to bear My name before Gentiles, kings, and the children of Israel. For I will show him how many things he must suffer for My name's sake." Love will face the adversary and convert him to a friend. Ananias went to Saul, ministered healing and Saul was then baptized. Only then did Saul eat and was strengthened. Afterwards, he spent several days with the Christians in the area. Going forth, he would now be persecuted by the same group who authorized him to carry out the previous persecutions of the church. Interesting!

Paul does not receive the fullness of his calling yet. He spent three years in Arabia "conferring not with flesh and blood" in order to prepare for his calling. He separated himself from the church and man's influence in order that his heart be cleansed and prepared for his ministry. He abode with Peter fifteen days. Afterwards, he was "commissioned" by the prophets and teachers to go forth. He was never called by his Hebrew name "Saul" again. From that point he was known as Paul.

Paul's encounter with Jesus Christ changed his world. His education in Hebrew law under the teaching of Gamaliel prepared him as a rabbi, teacher, and lawyer. He clearly excelled at his profession for he became a Roman citizen. But the event on the road to Damascus changed everything. He was baptized in the Holy Spirit and empowered by Our Heavenly Father to go forth and preach the Gospel to the Gentiles, a group of people he would have previously shunned. Paul received the revelation of Love. Love was not moved by his past life of persecuting and killing Christians. Grace and mercy prevailed in his life. He now walked according to Love rather than the letter and customs of the Law. He finally understood the Lawgiver and the character of Our Heavenly Father. Just as Jesus summed up the Law with Love so did Paul in Romans 13.

Paul expounds on the Ten Commandments and their relationship to Love:

> Romans 13:8 Owe no man any thing, but to love one another: for he that loveth another hath fulfilled the law.
> 9 For this, Thou shalt not commit adultery, Thou shalt not kill, Thou shalt not steal, Thou shalt not bear false witness, Thou shalt not covet; and if there be any other commandment, it is briefly comprehended in this saying, namely, Thou shalt love thy neighbour as thyself.
> 10 Love worketh no ill to his neighbour: therefore love is the fulfilling of the law.

What a contrast for the man who officiated over Stephen's death. Was there a price to pay for all the persecutions that he invoked? Yes. Love still demanded restitution for all of Paul's actions though he was spared death by Stephen's prayer. In 2 Corinthians 11, Paul reveals his exposure to adversity:

"in stripes above measure, in prisons more frequently, in deaths often. From the Jews five times I received forty stripes minus one. Three times I was beaten with rods; once I was stoned; three times I was shipwrecked; a night and a day I have been in the deep; in journeys often, in perils of waters, in perils of robbers, in perils of my own countrymen, in perils of the Gentiles, in perils in the city, in perils in the wilderness, in perils in the sea, in perils among false brethren; in weariness and toil, in sleeplessness often, in hunger and thirst, in fastings often, in cold and nakedness".

As an expert in the Law, he knew judgment, testing, and correction were needful. With the revelation of Love, he was able to see the importance of the adversities he suffered as he spread the Gospel of Love knowing that he was fully reconciled to Our Heavenly Father and that the sufferings of this present time are not worthy to be compared with the glory which shall be revealed in us. The judgment of Love prepares us for the glorification that is to come soon.

Personal Assessment:
1. Do you currently see yourself under judgment? If so, why?
2. Do you find yourself habitually breaking the Law of Love?
3. Are you planting seeds of division, alienation, and/or criticism?
4. What actions can you take to stop judgment on yourself or others?
5. What can you do to counteract greed?

Chapter 10
The Second Coming of Love

Let us revisit a simple and absolute truth:

> John 3:16 For God so loved the world, that he gave his only begotten Son, that whosoever believeth in him should not perish, but have everlasting life.

This was the first "Coming" of Jesus Christ. It represented a type and shadow to another "coming". Our Heavenly Father had four writers of the Gospels as well as Paul to document many of the words and works of Jesus. Those writings have survived 2,000 years. Historians of Science readily acknowledge that Jesus walked the earth, the evidence is without question. The principles of the New Testament have produced good fruit and countless miracles as further proof of the veracity of the first coming. Jesus told us that HE and Our Heavenly Father are one. John, aka the beloved disciple, had an insight of Love as expressed in this writings. These writings originated by the direct association with Our Lord Jesus Christ. John wrote:

> 1 John 4:8 He that loveth not knoweth not God; for God is love.

again...

> 1 John 4:16 And we have known and believed the love that God hath to us. God is love; and he that dwelleth in love dwelleth in God, and God in him.

He that dwelleth (stay, remain continually) in Love, dwelleth in God, and God in him. This is a powerful reality. If you remain immersed in Love, you are in God and God is in you. This is a simple and direct truth. We all want this reality but yet our focus tends to be on all other aspects of Scripture. We get caught up on less critical priorities rather than retain our focus on what should be the most important aspect of life, dwelling with Our Heavenly Father. Do you claim to know Our Heavenly Father? Do you claim to know Our Lord Jesus Christ? Be brutally honest with yourself. Are you pursuing a walk in Love or a walk based on self motivations designed to survive against your enemies with a willingness to compromise your stated beliefs if put in a highly stressful state? When all is well anybody can claim a Love walk. Your core beliefs rise to the surface when you are faced with unexpected, catastrophic situations. When your stress level exceeds the national debt, what is your response? Do you lash out at loved ones? Do you create an enemy to be attacked with words or actions? Jesus provides us the comparative analysis of Love's responses to the stress and pressures of life. As we transform into Love ourselves, we will begin to tap into the same power that created the universe, commanded miracles to come forth to meet the needs of the masses, and overcame death. The fulfillment of Love is glorification!

There has been much discussion about the gifts of the Holy Spirit as listed in 1 Corinthians 12:

The Word of Knowledge
The Word of Wisdom
The Gift of Prophecy
The Gift of Faith
The Gifts of Healings
The Working of Miracles
The Discerning of Spirits
Different Kinds of Tongues
The Interpretation of Tongues

Ascending to Love

These gifts have been exercised by the Pentecostal church along with many abuses. Were the miracles real? Absolutely! Did sin occur by the same men by whose hands did the miracles come forth? No doubt. The Feast of Weeks or Pentecost included "leavened" bread instead of unleavened bread used in the other two feasts:

> Leviticus 23:15 'And you shall count for yourselves from the day after the Sabbath, from the day that you brought the sheaf of the wave offering: seven Sabbaths shall be completed. 16 Count fifty days to the day after the seventh Sabbath; then you shall offer a new grain offering to the LORD. 17 You shall bring from your dwellings two wave loaves of two-tenths of an ephah. They shall be of fine flour; they shall be baked with leaven. They are the firstfruits to the LORD. (NKJV)

Leaven represents sin. Paul's letter to the Corinthians provides us with understanding about the problem of leaven. The church has both sin and miracles occurring at the same time and under the same roof. On one hand mighty miracles are in operation but at the same time sexual immorality is being reported among them. This immorality is not even named among the Gentiles! The church has a problem… as it does today. How can a man be baptized in the Holy Spirit with the evidence of speaking in other Tongues and be in sin as well? Our Heavenly Father knew this would be the case when HE instituted the second major feast of the year. This feast would be a type and shadow of the condition of the Church Age. Paul was compelled to deal with the leaven in the church at Corinth. He writes in Chapter 5:

> 6 Your glorying is not good. Do you not know that a little leaven leavens the whole lump?
> 7 Therefore purge out the old leaven, that you may be a new lump, since you truly are unleavened. For indeed Christ, our Passover, was sacrificed for us.

8 Therefore let us keep the feast, not with old leaven, nor with the leaven of malice and wickedness, but with the unleavened bread of sincerity and truth.

The word "glorying" means boasting in the context of associating it with leaven, or sin. Paul mentions all three feasts here: Christ, our Passover, the feast of old leaven (Pentecost), and the final feast again with unleavened bread (Tabernacles) based on sincerity and truth. This third feast continues to be my focus in writing on Love. I believe this to be Paul's focus as well. The church at Corinth is an excellent example of the church age we have been experiencing. Corruption has been found among the clergy, evangelists, teachers, etc. It seems that the sins of the church are continually exposed through the media. One would say it is a target-rich environment for news reporters. Does that discount all the good that has been done by the church? Absolutely not! Does that negate the salvation of millions? No!

Consider this: the gifts of the Holy Spirit are needed because there is need for correction, restoration, and reconciliation. Would you need the gift of healing if all were healed and in full command of their physiology? "Discerning of spirits" is needed because there are spiritual forces that need to be discerned. The Holy Spirit was given to us as our Comforter and with this impartation we are given a means to deal with adversity whether be sickness, disease, spiritual battles, or faith to overcome insurmountable odds. I am always amazed at people who discount the nine spiritual gifts given to us by Our Heavenly Father for the purpose of blessing those in need. They look at the abuses of those empowered with the gifts and discount the gifts themselves. That ought not to be. Jesus operated in spiritual gifts without measure. He was in full command of those gifts from the first day of His ministry.

Paul's ministry operated in the Spiritual Gifts as well thus he was justified in writing about their proper use. Our Heavenly Father would not have Paul pen those words unless Paul had full understanding of the gifts and their operation. The church was immature and self motivated. However, Paul did not threaten them with eternal hell. Instead, his letter was all about correction and restoration. He did not tell them to quit operating in the Gifts of the Holy Spirit but instead he urged them to move out of the Pentecost paradigm and move forward into the Tabernacles realm. In chapter 12 he starts out by explaining spiritual gifts and their proper operation. He puts order into their services. It would appear that men's egos were overtaking the services and creating chaos and confusion. Paul calls for unity among the brethren for it is clear they were not in one accord. He also stresses the point that one person's gifts and calling are not more important than another person's gifts and calling. The body has need of every part.

The last verse of this chapter provides an invaluable key that no one focuses on. Paul writes in verse 30, "But eagerly desire the greater gifts. And now I will show you the most excellent way."

The second coming of Christ has been dissected to the nth degree. John also wrote of this reality. We keep looking up in the sky rather than inward where the action is. As I wrote in The Circumcised Heart of Love, the fulfillment of the third and final feast will be a full immersion of Love also known as The Second Coming of Christ, the most excellent way.

Paul has just discussed the nine spirituals (gifts) of the Holy Spirit for which we are thankful. Having operated in some of these gifts at various and sundry times, I can personally attest to the blessing they have provided to those in attendance. The anointing of the Holy Spirit and the Word of Our Heavenly Father during the operation of those gifts provided specific words of encouragement, discerning of spirits, healings, supernatural faith, knowledge of the hidden things of the heart, and other impartations needed at the time. During a missionary trip to Romania, myself and two other men operated daily in this anointing and it did set the captives free. The miracles that resulted from the operation of these gifts became well known and people in need would seek us out to pray for their loved ones. However, the most excellent way had not come.

Paul was about to give the key to operating in a greater anointing than the Corinthians had experienced. Their anointing or empowerment had been mixed with sin but the path to the fullness of Christ was before them. He was ministering to them as a father, not as an instructor:

> 1 Corinthians 4:15 For though you might have ten thousand instructors in Christ, yet you do not have many fathers; for in Christ Jesus I have begotten you through the gospel. (NKJV)

A father is fully invested in the son's maturity for there is an inheritance involved. An instructor has an obligation to teach but does not necessarily teach from the motivation of Love. Paul establishes a relationship as a "father" to sons and daughters who have erred in their desire for the greater aspects of a spiritual walk. They were clearly open and sensitive to receiving the gifts of the Holy Spirit but failed in walking in a lawful manner. It would appear that the Law had been tossed out once the spiritual gifts had arrived. Who better than Paul who was an expert in the Mosaic Law give instruction as a father to those who were offering up sacrifices with leaven.

The most excellent way is Love, the consummation of the Law and the Spirit. Jesus operated in both and the Mount of Transfiguration provides us the example of this consummation. Moses who represented the Law and Elijah representing the Spirit joined Jesus who represents both were all in a transfigured state. This was prior to His death and resurrection, a key point. By Law, Jesus had to be subjected to humanity and overcome death. He embraced human form and all its characteristics in order to satisfy the Law of sacrifice. What does this mean to us? We have the same ability to transform as He did. Love fulfills the Law and the Spirit for out of the character of Our Heavenly Father came the Law and the Spirit. Love is that character!

In the 13th chapter of 1 Corinthians, Paul explains the most excellent way to the church. He describes sixteen attributes of Love though there are infinite ways to describe Love for it cannot be fit inside man's comprehension. Paul tells us that Love endures beyond all the gifts given to the church. Love was the intent behind the gifts thus it is inherently greater than any gift given. Just as Our Heavenly Father wants the best for HIS children, Paul wants the best for the church who has been operating in sin at the same time manifesting the spiritual gifts of the Holy Spirit.

Paul makes a bold statement:

> 1 Corinthians 13:2 And though I have the gift of prophecy, and understand all mysteries and all knowledge, and though I have all faith, so that I could remove mountains, but have not love, I am nothing. (KJV)

How many Christians focus on prophecy today? Every disaster provides the prophecy teachers move justification for their ministry. Christian television has provided some prophecy teachers with a platform for their ministry for decades. As a young man I recall that the return of Christ was imminent. He was prophesied to return in 1988, 1993, 1996, 1999, 2000, etc. I believe His Return is predicated on our revelation of Love. Paul urged us to focus on Love. John told us to focus on Love. And most of all, Jesus told us to focus on Love. Isn't it about time that we set aside the secondary topics that would divert our focus and preoccupy our time with less critical aspects of our callings. Now is the time to focus on Love. The fullness of Love is the Return of Christ.

Personal Assessment:
1. Do you believe that you are to be a part of the "second coming"?
2. Are you dwelling in Love more this month than last month?
3. Have you prayed to be used in the gifts of the Holy Spirit? In not, why not?
4. Do you believe that Our Heavenly Father is willing to expand His use of you to minister to mankind?
5. Do you find yourself dwelling on the future at the expense of the present?

Chapter 11

THE UNITY OF LOVE

"I and [my] Father are one." John 10:30

The Kingdom of Our Heavenly Father is one of unity. There is no division or dissention among the inhabitants of Heaven. They are all in one accord. The universe is in unity in that all of the stars and planets are kept in balance by the Spirit of GOD and they function in one accord on a daily basis. Thankfully, the planets are not colliding with each other but are held in their orbits as declared by the Creator of the universe. The preciseness of their orbits can be projected over millions of years with such reliability that we are in awe of the ancient stargazers and their ability to track the stars and planets. The vastness of the universe is a testimony to the unity in Heaven.

Jesus understood this attribute of Heaven. HE promoted unity and understood the destructiveness of division. "Every kingdom divided against itself is brought to desolation; and every city or house divided against itself shall not stand" was spoken by Jesus in response to accusations by the Pharisees. The Kingdom of GOD will not be brought to desolation. A primary characteristic and purpose of Our Heavenly Father is unity and restoration of a breach or division.

Over the years, church leaders interpreted Scripture to fulfill their agendas of control. What better control is there than the fear of hell and eternal damnation. This theory would suggest that Our Heavenly Father of Love has a flaw that allows man whom he created, to burn in hell. By preying on man's ignorance of Scripture and his emotional tendency to accept fear, leaders were able to keep their congregations in submission to their personal agendas. Rather than serve mankind they wanted to control the populace.

Love unites and unifies. When man and woman love each other and marry, they become "one" in unity. When people are in unity, peace prevails. The concept is so simple yet the application has been very elusive to most people. Why? It is because the ego has been the driving force and basis of man's actions. The ego divides and conquers whereas Love unites and reconciles.

This brings up a fundamental question about man. When did Jesus Christ enter into our being? When did the "zoe" life enter in? This question challenges most of the doctrines man has taught in the last 100 years. The evangelist would ask the question, "Would you like to ask Jesus into your heart today?" The question would infer that Jesus Christ is not there before the question is asked, but is He?

Is there anywhere where the Spirit of GOD is not? Did the Word of GOD create everything and give life to all living things? How can every particle in our body have intelligence to carry out its assigned function? Doesn't intelligence precede assignment? There must be some type of "glue" that holds all of the GOD particles in the universe together.

The ego would have us believe that we are independent life forms from Our Heavenly Father. Mankind has attempted to explain away the beginning of the universe and the beginning of life forms by some inanimate, random occurrence without any intelligent, guiding involvement. When one studies the physical sciences at the micro level and studies astronomy at the macro level, it does not take a brilliant mind to conclude that a superior intelligence created the universe. Only those who are blinded and without wisdom and understanding could draw such a conclusion of random occurrence!

From anywhere on earth and at any time of the day, men pray to Our Heavenly Father. There is no place on earth where HE is not. There are countless examples of prayers being answered instantaneously 10,000 miles away. In order to mature in our understanding of the unity of Love we must accept that fact there is no "nothingness". Our eyes would have us believed that the space between two objects contains nothing even though we can intelligently conclude that air is filled with oxygen that sustains our lives and the carbon dioxide we exhale makes its way to plants for their benefit. We also understand radio waves, light waves, and other wave forms passing through this space that is undetectable by the eye. Why is it so hard to comprehend the intelligence of the Holy Spirit is occupying this space at a frequency superior to our ability to detect with the five natural senses?

Another major obstacle we must overcome is the paradigm of time. The essence of time is division. It allows us to differentiate experiences, slice up events and plans into unique thoughts, and provides us benchmarks of progress. The older we become, the shorter the day gets. Time is useful but it is not the fullness of our being, infinity is. To conclude our being ends with physical death is to disregard all aspects of observations, scientific discoveries, and credible testimonies of those who were clinically dead and return to their physical bodies. Our ego would attempt to disregard all the evidence in favor of its temporary control of your focus.

One of the most abstract realities our mind attempts to grasp is infinity. Living in the time continuum, we are oriented to finite understanding. A day lasts 24 hours, a foot is measured to 12 inches, etc. We observe a four dimensional world of length, width, depth, and time. However, a circle allows us to comprehend infinity to a degree for it has no beginning or end. You could go in a circle indefinitely and never come to a conclusion. You could travel for infinity. Our Heavenly Father created time and is not defined by it. HE created the four dimensions we observe as well as other dimensions we are now discovering. The unifying aspect of all these dimensions is Our Heavenly Father Who is Love. Love is the glue that holds all things together. Our Heavenly Father created mathematics and that discipline allows us to grasp infinity. By simply adding one to the next number no matter how great, infinity is expressed. Additionally by finding a number between any two numbers expresses infinity at the other end of the scale.

The intent of Love expressed itself in a many faceted form. Love created a dialogue which appeared to be division but never sacrificed unity. Just as in marriage, two are one, and one is made of two without sacrificing unity. Marriage allows us to view a unity from two perspectives, male and female. Each has different tendencies and views that produce a dialogue of completeness and unity. Love provides that bond. When the ego jumps into the equation on either side, strife and contention occur and unfortunately ends up in divorce. Jesus made it very clear that division is destructive:

> Matthew 11:25 But Jesus knew their thoughts, and said to them: "Every kingdom divided against itself is brought to desolation, and every city or house divided against itself will not stand." (NKJV)

Most Christians can quote John 3:16 but verse 17 further explains the unity of Love:

> 17 For God did not send His Son into the world to condemn the world, but that the world through Him might be saved. (NKJV)

Condemnation precedes death and destruction which is contrary to the intent of Love. Love saves and restores. The word saved is the Greek word "sozo". It means: to save, keep safe and sound, to rescue from danger or destruction, from injury or peril; to save a suffering one from perishing, i.e. one suffering from disease, to make well, heal, restore to health. This was Jesus' mandate: to restore, to make whole. This mandate was given by Our Creator and it is clear that Our Heavenly Father would provide a complete mandate that allowed for all to be saved without exception. The self-serving ego would be the only challenge to this reality. The ego of men would attempt to divide and enslave others in order to perpetuate control but only for short period of time. The emptiness of the ego has been witnessed by each of us in our own failures. On the other hand, acts of Love perpetuate peace and fellowship. Each and every one of us is called to initiate acts of Love as well as embrace Love. This creates a stereophonic effect of beauty that is beheld as Love goes forth. The fundamental family unit is a microcosm of this effect. When the sunset is beheld by a couple who communicate its beauty, the experience is multiplied beyond what one person perceives when observing the same event alone. There is a certain fulfillment of Love when two or more people share an experience of beauty, excitement, or revelation.

There is no limit to unity. When a group of people come together in unity, their power increases in a exponential manner. A large boulder needs to be rolled away. A skyscraper needs to be built. When men and women come together in unity, the challenges become manageable and success is achieved by unity. On the other hand, division ensures failure. The Tower of Babel was a perfect example of unity versus division:

> Genesis 11:5 But the LORD came down to see the city and the tower which the sons of men had built.
> 6 And the LORD said, "Indeed the people are one and they all have one language, and this is what they begin to do; now nothing that they propose to do will be withheld from them.
> 7 Come, let Us go down, and there confuse their language, that they may not understand one another's speech." (NKJV)

After the flood, Our Heavenly Father made a commitment to Noah and his descendents that HE would not flood the earth again. The unrighteous self interests had escalated to the point where the earth needed cleansed. Unity motivated by perverse behavior can also take advantage of the exponential growth to a conclusion. To remove this fleshly ability to unify the whole earth, Our Heavenly Father placed a barrier by creating multiple languages. This insured that unification by the Spirit would be the only way for people to totally achieve all they proposed to do. Unity by the Spirit is a good thing. Unity based on self interest is ultimately destructive and if this destructiveness filled the earth again, mutual destruction is all but assured.

Ascending to Love

The Old Testament Law promoted unity among all groups of people: the spouse, the brother, the neighbor, the worker, and the afflicted. In Leviticus 19:

> 11 'You shall not steal, nor deal falsely, nor lie to one another.
> 12 And you shall not swear by My name falsely, nor shall you profane the name of your God: I am the LORD.
> 13 'You shall not cheat your neighbor, nor rob him. The wages of him who is hired shall not remain with you all night until morning.
> 14 You shall not curse the deaf, nor put a stumbling block before the blind, but shall fear your God: I am the LORD.
> 15 You shall do no injustice in judgment. You shall not be partial to the poor, nor honor the person of the mighty. In righteousness you shall judge your neighbor.
> 16 You shall not go about as a talebearer among your people; nor shall you take a stand against the life of your neighbor: I am the LORD.
> 17 You shall not hate your brother in your heart. You shall surely rebuke your neighbor, and not bear sin because of him.
> 18 You shall not take vengeance, nor bear any grudge against the children of your people, but you shall love your neighbor as yourself: I am the LORD. (NKJV)

The Israelites had been in bondage under the Egyptians and had taken on their values since their own had been suppressed. Earlier generations had been given the opportunity to live righteously under the direction of Our Heavenly Father but had rejected it in order to serve their own flesh, much to their dismay. This new generation needed training and understanding much like a child needed a set of rules until the child could reason for himself. The immaturity of the mass of people required the 613 commandments and statutes until Love arrived in Bethlehem. The master plan to restore mankind in Love thus reducing the commandments to just two would require the physical manifestation of Jesus to walk the earth. Our Heavenly

Father would express Himself in a lower physical form in order that mankind could comprehend the Love of the Creator. This example should serve as evidence that Our Heavenly Father will stop at nothing to bring for the Unity of Love to all of mankind.

Personal Assessment:
1. Do you promote unity or division?
2. What have you done lately to remove alienation from others which were caused by your actions?
3. Do you promote inclusiveness or an air of entitlement and separation?
4. What percentage of interaction with others can you attribute to listening?
5. What percentage of your conversation would you directly attribute to speaking only the words you hear Our Heavenly Father speak?

Chapter 12
The Authority of Love

> "Then Jesus called His twelve disciples together and gave them power and authority over all demons, and to cure diseases."

In Luke Chapter 9, we find that Love gives power and authority. This is a monumental revelation to those who would grasp the ramifications of this verse. We also find in Psalm 62, "God has spoken once, Twice I have heard this: That power belongs to God". All power originates from Our Heavenly Father who is Love. In John 19 Jesus flatly tells Pilate, "You could have no power at all against Me unless it had been given you from above". Our Heavenly Father gave HIS Son power which in turn was imparted to the disciples. This power has dominion over the spiritual, mental, emotional, and physical aspects of all life. The power of Love is primal and creative and every aspect of the universe must submit to this power.

Power without authority becomes lawless as the power is abused. Authority without power is frustrating at best when confronting the adversities that must be dealt with. When you have both power and authority, change will occur.

Authority is the delegated right to act in a specified way whereas power is the ability to do something or act in a particular way. Since Love created the Heavens and the earth and everything within, Love has the primal authority over all life and existence. The Creator is the first and ultimate authority over creation. All power originates from the intent of Our Heavenly Father who created every particle from the primal intent of Love.

"Talitha cumi!" Jesus spoke those two words and restored life to a twelve year old girl. He did not spend hours pleading with Our Heavenly Father to give Him the power to raise the dead. He didn't perform some mystical ceremony in a ritualistic fashion to summon life back to the girl, He just spoke two words backed by both power and authority. Love has power over death just as it has power over sickness and disease. The particles that make up our existence are all subject to the command of Love. When in disorder and chaos, the particles respond to the command to return to order, the state of their original intent. Our minds have been bombarded with the belief that sickness and disease are a necessary evil of life and that we should simply cope with that "reality". We have been convinced by the media that sickness is a lack of some pharmaceutical drug and that we should take pills the rest of our life to insure a quality state of existence. Nothing is further from the truth. Jesus did not call some pharmacy for drugs to heal the woman with the issue of blood! Pharmaceuticals have replaced Love, faith, and hope in the daily lives of many. As we turn to the revelation of Love, I expect the power and authority over sickness and disease to be given to those who have been proven trustworthy to receive such a service to the multitudes.

Chapter 5 of the Gospel of Mark contains important aspects of both power and authority when they operate by Love. The Mosaic Law called for no contact with any unclean or dead person yet Jesus in the same day dealt with both. When you operate in Love, you fulfill the Law. Uncleanness is overtaken by the cleansing and healing aspect of Love. Death is swallowed up by Love. Within the chapter of restoration and healing is another reference to the operational aspects of Divine government. Both the lady and the young girl's infirmities had culminated in twelve years, the Biblical number of Divine government. In the Old Testament, you were subject to sickness, disease, death, and their effects. But in the New Testament operating in Love, you are in command of all forms of death and disease, thus you are not subject to their effects. When Love arrives, death departs!

The word "authority" is first mentioned in the New Testament in the Gospel of Matthew chapter 7. Jesus is teaching the various

Ascending to Love

aspects of the Kingdom. He is providing practical examples of those who operate according to Kingdom principles and those who don't. With these examples, the average person can discern who is and who isn't. Jesus makes a very poignant statement to some:

> 21 "Not everyone who says to Me, 'Lord, Lord,' shall enter the kingdom of heaven, but he who does the will of My Father in heaven. (NKJV)

There are those who profess to have power and authority and proclaim Jesus is Lord but will not enter the kingdom of heaven. Why? They did not do the will of Our Heavenly Father. What is His will? To walk in Love. Jesus summed up the entire Law by Love and that IS the will of Our Heavenly Father. By HIS will did HE establish the Law! Jesus started the chapter with "Judge not, that you be not judged" for judging causes division, not restoration.

Ask, and it shall be given you; seek, and ye shall find; knock, and it shall be opened unto you. When we seek Our Heavenly Father we are told to ask, seek, and knock. Seek what? There is a portal or door in each of us with direct access to Our Heavenly Father. It is the entrance to the Holy of Holies inside of us where the ark of the Covenant resides. The Key of David (Love) opens that portal. As we passionately pursue that portal, we will receive the "gift" of revelation and operation of this power and authority of Love that will allow us to fully serve mankind as Jesus did. How much more will your Father who is in heaven give good things to those who ask Him!

Jesus then provides us perspective about this walk of Love:

> 13 "Enter by the narrow gate; for wide is the gate and broad is the way that leads to destruction, and there are many who go in by it.
> 14 Because narrow is the gate and difficult is the way which leads to life, and there are few who find it. (NKV)

It is not an easy road to take and there will be notable challenges. Our ego and flesh want us to take the broad and easy path to destruction. Our ego wants to control us and lead us down the path of arrogance, idols, and entitlement. Our flesh wants us to wallow around in lasciviousness. The walk of Love is not the popular walk with many Christian doctrines. "Turn or burn" is their motto. Those churches would have us all believe that the primal characteristic of Our Heavenly Father would somehow create people who would sin so that HE would condemn them to eternal punishment. If they fully understood Love, they would immediately search those Scriptures out to find the real translation and the intent behind them. They use a couple of misinterpretations to build an entire doctrine of entitlement. They will be the ones who plead "Lord, Lord".

How are we to guard ourselves against those who would lead us astray by false doctrines? Jesus answers this:

> 15 "Beware of false prophets, who come to you in sheep's clothing, but inwardly they are ravenous wolves.
> 16 You will know them by their fruits. (NKJV)

In Matthew 24:24 Jesus warns us, "For there shall arise false Christs, and false prophets, and shall show great signs and wonders; insomuch that, if it were possible, they shall deceive the very elect". Clearly we must be on guard against the false prophets and their deception. They perform great signs and wonders yet they are false prophets. What fruit should we be looking for? Love and all its attributes. When we seek the Character of Our Heavenly Father in men, we know the source of their power and authority. By the above warning, we know there is a counterfeit power that can deceive us. We must judge the fruit.

> Proverbs 29:2 When the righteous are in authority, the people rejoice; But when a wicked man rules, the people groan. (NKJV)

This Scripture provides us with a broad view of the fruit inspection. Is the population of the country rejoicing? This is not true in the U.S. as I suspect there is no other country that is currently rejoicing over its leadership. When those in authority serve mankind, the people have something to rejoice about.

Faith is also interwoven into the authority of Love. With authority, there is faith in the power that supports it for authority without power confirming it is impotent. Jesus had entered Capernaum, the house of the Comforter (Holy Spirit). A centurion of the Roman army heard of His arrival. The centurion had a slave who was at the point of death and sent word to Jesus to heal the servant:

> Luke 7:3 The centurion heard of Jesus and sent some elders of the Jews to him, asking him to come and heal his servant.
> 4 When they came to Jesus, they pleaded earnestly with him, "This man deserves to have you do this,
> 5 because he loves our nation and has built our synagogue."
> 6 So Jesus went with them. (NIV)

Does this man in authority cause the people to rejoice? He was loved by the Jewish elders because he served the community by building a synagogue. He loved their nation! Jesus was sent to the House of Israel but that did not prevent Him from ministering to the gentiles. Jesus responded to Love.

The centurion sent word to Jesus not to come for he was undeserving, but asked Him to simply speak the Word and the servant would be restored. The centurion understood faith in power and authority because he operated in it every day. Jesus marveled at the centurion's faith and stated, "I tell you, I have not found such great faith even in Israel." Immediately, the servant was healed. Time and distance was not an issue to Jesus nor the healing power and authority He possessed.

Our Heavenly Father assigns positions of authority in the Kingdom, no one else. In Matthew chapter 20, the mother of James and John came with her sons and requested that they be placed in authority, one to sit at His right hand and the other to sit at His left hand in His Kingdom. Jesus told them that they did not know what they were asking. He replied, "to sit on My right hand and on My left is not Mine to give, but it is for those for whom it is prepared by My Father." Our Heavenly Father assigns our gifts, callings, power, and authority thus we must operate within those assignments. Any attempt to operate outside of your calling will only result in failure. If you don't have a financial calling, quit trying to usurp those who do. If you are not called to be a prophet, don't try to muster up a prophetic word to draw attention to yourself for that is your ego at work in all its subtleness.

Jesus summarized Kingdom authority:

25 But Jesus called them to Himself and said, "You know that the rulers of the Gentiles lord it over them, and those who are great exercise authority over them.
26 Yet it shall not be so among you; but whoever desires to become great among you, let him be your servant.
27 And whoever desires to be first among you, let him be your slave—
28 just as the Son of Man did not come to be served, but to serve, and to give His life a ransom for many." NKJV

You weren't born to be served but were brought forth to serve mankind with your gifts and calling in Love.

Your fruitfulness is a sign of your power and authority. What skills do you have that blesses mankind? Every gift and calling has a GOD-given power inherent in it to cause fruit to come forth. Your calling is ordained from the Throne room of Heaven and that is the source of the power and authority from which you operate. You must relax in that reality. John the Baptist was a prophet whose fruit was judged by the people to be good. His authority came from Our Heavenly Father. Signs and wonders will follow the calling. People will marvel at your ability to produce fruit in the area of your skill set and passion. Whether you are a trim carpenter who can build a beautiful

Ascending to Love

kitchen from scratch, or a marketing representative that people are attracted to, your calling will become clear.

Over the years, people have given the devil too much credit. They speak as though satan was omnipresent and plaguing all men simultaneously. Spiritual rulers of darkness need darkness in order to rule. Love shines the light on any matter but if you persist in assigning power and authority to darkness, you have effectively agreed with those powers. Where men have pursued lawlessness, darkness has prevailed. Habitual lawlessness establishes strongholds of darkness. However mature Love will break those strongholds and remove the darkness swiftly and effectively. Jesus provided us an excellent example of swift restoration in Luke 4:

> 31 Then He went down to Capernaum, a city of Galilee, and was teaching them on the Sabbaths.
> 32 And they were astonished at His teaching, for His word was with authority.

The people perceived His fullness of understanding of the Word of GOD. His revelation caused them to be astonished. He clearly was teaching the principles of Love, the culmination of The Law. Once Love was revealed as the intent behind the Law, darkness knew that it was a matter of time before men would remove the authority of darkness in their lives. This called for drastic measures by a demon:

> 33 Now in the synagogue there was a man who had a spirit of an unclean demon. And he cried out with a loud voice,
> 34 saying, "Let us alone! What have we to do with You, Jesus of Nazareth? Did You come to destroy us? I know who You are—the Holy One of God!"
> 35 But Jesus rebuked him, saying, "Be quiet, and come out of him!" And when the demon had thrown him in their midst, it came out of him and did not hurt him.
> 36 Then they were all amazed and spoke among themselves, saying, "What a word this is! For with authority and power

He commands the unclean spirits, and they come out."
37 And the report about Him went out into every place in the surrounding region. (NKJV)

When Love spoke, darkness submitted! Jesus did not spend three hours of gut-wrenching, hand-wringing pleading to Our Heavenly Father to intervene on His behalf. He simply spoke with both power and authority. Love commands, darkness controls. The difference is clear.

When we operate in our calling and walk in Love, we have all the necessary power and authority to bring forth fruitfulness for all to judge. There is nothing that the authority of Love cannot overcome for Love has command over the entire universe. As we become mature in our revelation of Love, we will operate in the power and authority of Love for there in none greater.

Personal Assessment:
1. What portion of your discretionary time do you spend serving versus being served?
2. Do you project an air of entitlement?
3. How do you treat servers at a restaurant?
4. Think of someone who serves you. What can you do for him or her as a service?
5. Find a few strangers and do something of service for them.

Chapter 13
The Acceptance of Love

To accept Love is to accept your destiny and surrender your mind, will, and emotions to Love. Your ego must be put in its place once and for all. Your mind must become the servant it was designed to be. Your emotions must not rule the day but must be allowed to be expressed in innocence. Your will must submit to your destiny also known as your calling. You have been given the choice to accept or reject Love. Love demands choice to be given to all of its children.

Stop blaming your circumstances as the reason you have failed to walk in your calling. Our Heavenly Father gave you all the necessary gifts to walk in your calling. Failure to walk in the destiny you have been called to is due to your decisions to stray from that calling, often induced by your ego. Your ego is your accuser. Your ego will tell you to manipulate others then later condemn you for it so that you will feel to unworthy to go before the Throne of Grace to receive mercy and restoration by Our Heavenly Father. Your ego will entice you to lie about the circumstances which you face in order to maintain control, exalt yourself, or divert punishment away from you even though it is well deserved.

Walk in humility, not in pride. You must humble yourself, not in false humility, but in a genuine walk that is not self-promoting in nature. False humility is simply a manipulative effort of projecting yourself to others as achieving a pure state without requiring your ego to submit to your spirit. You are lying to yourself.

Ascending to Love means that you will start identifying with Our Heavenly Father just as a child identifies with the earthly father by imitating the father's actions and character. Once you begin to relate to Love, restoration begins. The process is not pleasant to our flesh by any means. The Scripture provides many examples of the process and one of the most direct examples of Joseph, the son of Jacob.

Joseph went through a thirteen year training period to fulfill his calling or destiny, one in Potiphar's house and twelve in prison. He didn't just wake up one day and ascend to the number two position in Egypt. Instead, he needed to be prepared for his calling and all of us must go through this preparation. Many of us relate with Joseph because his journey reminds us of our own trials and tests in route to our calling.

Awareness of our calling may come by a prophetic word sent by Our Heavenly Father, whether it was sent through a family member or someone with a prophetic calling. When we receive the witness in our spirit of that Word, we get excited. Our excitement turns to pride and arrogance that is fueled by our immaturity. Joseph provided us with an excellent example of immature pride when he boasted to his older brothers of the prophetic word of them bowing down to him. He did not win a popularity test that day. His pride caused him to end up in a pit. Are you in a pit? Quit griping about your pit and ask the simple question: Why? This question allows you to move forward in ascending to your calling of Love. Acceptance of instruction by Our Heavenly Father brings forth your destiny in each situation you are placed. The pit is where you learn what impact pride can have.

Jesus also went through a twelve plus one year training period. When Jewish boys reach 13, they become responsible for their actions and become a Bar Mitzvah "coming of age". In Luke 2:42 we are told the story of Jesus being twelve years and six months at Passover. He was entering the age of accountability. This is the Scripture's only reference to Him as a youth and this is when He proclaimed that He must be about His Father's business. Jesus dealt with the ego and made himself of no reputation, and took upon him the form of a servant, and was made in the likeness of men to the point of becoming obedient unto death.

We are not to be jealous of others' gifts and callings but to accept the reality of our calling to bless mankind. Joseph's brothers were envious of his calling and were concerned about their inheritance from their father. They were insecure in their relationship and had no faith that Our Heavenly Father would provide for them.

In order to ascend to a mature state of Love, *your character must be developed and tested.* You must learn stewardship and become a servant just as Jesus took on no reputation. You must become obedient to the death of your ego. Joseph's pride took him to the pit, the opposite direction of his calling. We often think that we will go in a straight line to fulfill our calling but that is never the case. Our path will often parallel that of Joseph for we must pass several character tests before we can enter into the fullness of our calling.

After Joseph's dream, he became a "wandering generality". He knew his calling but had no idea how it was going to come to pass. Had he know what he was about to go through, he would have probably not accepted the calling but run in the opposite direction. Jacob had sent him to find his brothers and Joseph was wandering in a field when a "certain" man found him and directed him to his brothers. I would suggest that this "certain" man was a messenger of Our Heavenly Father. Joseph wore his calling for all to see. Obviously the coat of many colors was easily seen from a distance. Our ego gets us excited about being exalted in our calling and causes us to be seen as arrogant to our brethren. Joseph was no different. His brothers could see him coming and conspired to kill him. Reuben, the oldest, stopped him and prevented his death. Instead, Reuben compelled them to throw Joseph into the pit. Joseph's pride put him into the pit and this became a time of reflection for the seventeen year-old. His character began its development. Often we blame other people for our place in the pit when our ego is the culprit. For the next thirteen years, Joseph would learn through the character-building opportunities he would face. His faith in the dream given to him by Our Heavenly Father would sustain him even in the pit.

Paul writes: "But we also glory in tribulations, knowing that tribulation produces perseverance; and perseverance, character; and character, hope. Now hope does not disappoint, because the love of

God has been poured out in our hearts by the Holy Spirit who was given to us." (Romans 5:3-5)

Clearly Joseph was in the beginning of his time of tribulation and was expecting to die from the lack of food and water. His dream was about to die. Only the hope of his calling would sustain him. In the meantime his brothers deceived his father of his whereabouts. Jacob chose to believe the lie over the assurance of the Joseph's calling. His ego once again got in the way of his relationship with Our Heavenly Father. Jacob was blind to the other sons' motives. You can be assured that Joseph cried out to Our Heavenly Father and pleaded with HIM about his circumstance. You can also be assured that Joseph asked forgiveness of his pride and arrogance and was willing to commit to anything in order to be saved from the pit. He got his wish.

As we accept the walk of Love, we are called to be stewards referring to a responsibility to take care of something belonging to someone else. A steward acts in a manner as though he owns whatever he is managing. A good steward pays attention to those details that determine success or failure and does not act in a reckless or trivial manner and he always acts in the best interest of the owner even if it is at a personal sacrifice. Good stewardship does not guarantee success of a project if others have a greater influence over it than the steward. However, the chances of success dramatically improve when the steward is involved versus an immature, poor steward who only has self promotion at heart. Good stewardship takes time to prove. A great steward will emulate his master to the point where he knows his master's mind, character, and intent, and will carry out his every wish just as though the master was providing direct supervision at every turn.

"For the kingdom of heaven is as a man travelling into a far country, who called his own servants, and delivered unto them his goods." In Matthew chapter 25, Jesus teaches us the parable of the talents. The stewardship test is specific to our gifts and calling thus each servant was given a varying number of talents, "to every man according to his several ability". The owner then departs into a far country which is an indication that the steward is free to do whatever he desires on a daily basis with nobody looking over his shoulder. Emotions are initially high when given the newly acquired responsibility of stewarding over someone else's money. "Look at me!" says the ego. Commitment is what is left after the emotion of the moment wears off. Once the fanfare subsides the steward is now to be tested. Will he take off a few days on a personal retreat or will he embrace stewardship and get to work on behalf of the master. How much of "self" will rule in the daily duties of the steward? Upon the owner's return, he rewards the good stewards with more. The poor steward failed the test and that which he had was taken from him and given to the good steward. Poor stewardship starts the training all over again. The Ishmeelites by way of the Midianites (strife and confusion) had sold Joseph to Potiphar as a slave. Joseph then ascended to the job of chief steward over Potiphar's house. His gifts were in full operation as he acted in the best interest of Potiphar. As an officer of Pharaoh and captain of the guard, Potiphar understood authority and responsibility and recognized those attributes in Joseph and he could see the favor of the LORD on him. Joseph was leading a pretty good life until it was time for his next test: purity of heart.

To be an overcomer, you must overcome something. It is easily concluded that Joseph was a good looking guy and Potiphar's wife cast longing eyes on Joseph. I am sure that she stroked his ego on a daily basis by flirting with him and tempting his heart. However, Joseph did not lift up his eyes to behold his master's wife. In Matthew 5:28 Jesus shares a truth about lust: "But I say to you that whoever looks at a woman to desire her has already committed adultery with her in his heart." The act of looking begins the cycle of lust, then adultery. Impurity begins with the eyes and the ego will tell you that looking is simply admiring beauty. It will always attempt to compromise the truth and steer you away from purity for the ego knows "Blessed are the pure in heart, for they will see God". And once you see Love face to face, it's all over for the ego. The ego will try to bend, twist, or distort the reality of being pure in an effort to maintain control. As we refrain from "lifting our eyes to behold" the temptation set before us, we protect our hearts from lust. Hollywood understands the subtle addiction to lust and attempts to capitalize on it by use of provocative scenes that excite the senses. Each of us must guard ourselves against the impurities of the world.

> Proverbs 27:20 Hell and Destruction are never full; So the eyes of man are never satisfied. (NKJV)

We must flee from sexual immorality. Jesus said in Matthew 6 22 "The lamp of the body is the eye. If therefore your eye is good, your whole body will be full of light. 23 But if your eye is bad, your whole body will be full of darkness. If therefore the light that is in you is darkness, how great is that darkness!" Our eyes begin the process and we must guard them to pass the purity test. As the external moves inward the war will rage on until it is either cleansed of unrighteousness or the lust is fulfilled. Our Savior provides the solution. The Law was put into effect to deal with transgressions, or outward actions. Iniquity is an inward motivation toward sin and must be dealt with by the Holy Spirit who will expose the lust in our hearts. In Isaiah 53:5 Jesus was wounded for our transgressions (external), he was bruised for our iniquities (internal). HE dealt with both aspects.

Even though Joseph passed the test of purity, he was not yet ready to fulfill his calling. He was now to be in prison for twelve years. This would now test his perseverance to accept his calling of Love for all mankind. He would spend time with the most rejected people of society: prisoners. The fullness of lawlessness was represented in the very place Joseph was required to stay for twelve long years. When Jesus died for the ungodly, we rarely consider who all that includes. Few of us have had a prison ministry where we have seen the transformation of criminals into saints. The Spirit of GOD is everywhere, even the darkest jail cell. Joseph was called to persevere through the lowest level of life in order to appreciate the task he was called to oversee. His perseverance test yielded positive results for he once again ascended to a position of stewardship. Your gifts will draw you to your calling like a magnet no matter where you end up. Joseph had to learn obedience through his suffering just as Jesus did.

Men and women will lie about you in order to satisfy their lusts. Their lies will challenge your perseverance and commitment to accept the walk of Love. They may sue you as a mean to manipulate you into compromising your commitment to walk upright and in righteousness. They may falsely accuse to divert your attention from your calling and get you to retaliate so as to justify their acts. When Jesus was accused, he became silent. False accusations will be dealt with by Our Heavenly Father. As we mature, we will no longer find it necessary to respond to those injustices done to us but will see those situations as character-building opportunities. Our character supports our destiny and character is developed by trials, deep character is learned through deep trials. Deep character flaws will be exposed and must be dealt with.

The development of character produces hope and hope is for "now". Hope deferred makes the heart sick, but when the desire comes, it is a tree of life. The tree of life has healing contained within its leaves. Our character tests can and will create wounds and bruising of their own. Love heals those wounds and bruises through forgiveness. Otherwise, those open sores will become roots of bitterness. Patience is waiting with contentment and we must let patience have its perfect work. As a young man I was impatient to achieve my goals and if I were told I would have to wait years for some prophetic event to occur I would be disappointed. Over the years I came to appreciate the need for patience to develop a maturity required for my calling. Since we are called to be steadfast and not moved by circumstances, patience is at the core of our development. Murmuring and complaining seems to extend your time of development.

Joseph did not get bitter about his circumstances. His thirteen year development plan was definitely extensive. He was required to persevere through harsh circumstances which molded his character and prepared him for his calling of service to mankind. Joseph had to be steadfast in his commitment to his calling for he knew the truth and Love that encapsulated that calling. All other voices had to be muted as they would try to convince him that his calling was not real. Perseverance required him to be strong and of good courage. We must remember that strength is needed when resistance is present. Courage is needed when adversity presents itself in the path you have been told to pursue thus we are told to resist the devil and he will flee. As we stand for truth and righteousness, the adversary is as a toothless lion with only a roar hoping to bluff your senses with fear. Paul shares, "Not that I speak in regard to need, for I have learned in whatever state I am, to be content." He then continues:

> Philippians 4: 12 I know how to be abased, and I know how to abound. Everywhere and in all things I have learned both to be full and to be hungry, both to abound and to suffer need 13 I can do all things through Christ who strengthens me. (NKJV)

Christ and HIS anointing of Love was sufficient for Paul as it is also sufficient for us today. Paul understood the need for patience and perseverance. He waited thirteen years to go on his first missionary trip. David waited thirteen years to reign over Israel. Joseph went through a thirteen year exhaustive course in character development before the fullness of his calling was to take effect.

Pain is a necessity of life. It produces an awareness that directs our focus to an area of need and correction. A headache is due to an inflammation that occurs from an unwelcomed arrival of a chemical or some other toxic agent to our system. The pain alerts us that a problem exists, which is good. This creates a response to correct the problem and move back to normality. Pain also gives us an appreciation for normality once it subsides.

> John 15:1 "I am the true vine, and My Father is the vinedresser. 2 Every branch in Me that does not bear fruit He takes away; [fn1] and every branch that bears fruit He prunes, that it may bear more fruit. (NKJV)

In John 15, the branch either gets cut or cut off but either way a cut will occur. This is an important reality to embrace. We have

Ascending to Love

become so adverse to pain and suffering that we will often do anything to avoid it. It is like avoiding a root canal to avoid pain at the cost of losing the tooth. As we mature we understand the necessity of pain and suffering as part of the maturing process. We must not pursue pain as though it in itself is necessary but understand that it is simply part of the process. As we are enduring the pain in the process of maturing, our hope must remain intact and Love is there to insure this:

> Romans 5:5 Now hope does not disappoint, because the love of God has been poured out in our hearts by the Holy Spirit who was given to us.

The pruning process builds a stronger plant and the unproductive, unfruitful parts of the plant are removed. We often acquire things in our lives that only serve to enslave us. Those things suck the life and resources out of our very existence. Young couples tend to buy a house beyond their means and become a slave to the exorbitant monthly payments. Their ego is temporarily satisfied but after the newness of the house wears off, they are simply saddled with an enslaving debt. The ego is a harsh taskmaster. Jesus' parable of the vine in John 15 reveals the need for pain in removing unproductive actions, acquisitions, and attitudes from us. Yes, our ego will suffer as it is removed from its exalted state in our lives. Joseph's brash attitude had to be pruned before he could ascend to his position of authority.

> Psalm 105:16 Moreover He called for a famine in the land; He destroyed all the provision of bread.
> 17 He sent a man before them—Joseph—who was sold as a slave.
> 18 They hurt his feet with fetters, He was laid in irons.
> 19 Until the time that his word came to pass, the Word of the LORD tested him. (NKJV)

The Word of the LORD will test us also. Everyone wants the excitement of a prophetic Word of the LORD until they realize the tests that will come forth associated with that Word. Joseph would not have been as boastful to his brothers about his calling had he known what the next thirteen years would require of him. Your calling will always have a series of tests associated with it! The prophetic Word tests our faith, the written Word tests our character.

The words of the LORD are pure words: as silver tried in a furnace of earth, purified seven times. Seven times!!! It sounds like our testing will be exhausting at times. Purification denotes the reality of flaws and impurities beforehand. As for God, His way is perfect; the word of the LORD is proven; He is a shield to all who trust in Him. Purity and perfection is needed at the zenith of your calling. His purification process was commensurate with the depth of his calling. Would you want any less of a man placed in authority to see you through a seven year famine?

Like Joseph, we all must keep the Words of the LORD before us. We must encourage ourselves that HE is faithful in every Word HE speaks. HE did not give us our calling by accident or without sovereign intent. The gifts HE placed within our essence were not without a reason. When we are in the midst of our trials, we must dwell on this reality and refrain from speaking against the Word that established our calling:

> Proverbs 4:20 My son, give attention to my words; Incline your ear to my sayings.
> 21 Do not let them depart from your eyes; keep them in the midst of your heart;
> 22 For they are life to those who find them, and health to all their flesh.
> 23 Keep your heart with all diligence, for out of it spring the issues of life.
> 24 Put away from you a deceitful mouth, and put perverse lips far from you.

Ascending to Love

Another pitfall preventing us from ascending to the fullness of our calling is to be guided by signs as our primary indicator to take action. Deuteronomy 13:1-5 provides us an explicit warning about prophetic signs. Judgment will come: "And that prophet, or that dreamer of dreams, shall be put to death; because he hath spoken to turn you away from the LORD your God". As Our Heavenly Father once explained to me, "All signs were created by ME but all are not relevant to you." Our Heavenly Father may use signs as confirmations and will alert you when they are applicable.

> Acts 2:2 And suddenly there came a sound from heaven as of a rushing mighty wind, and it filled all the house where they were sitting. KJV

In one day, you can be placed in the fullness of your calling. The disciples had been given the command by Our Lord to wait for the Holy Spirit. They had been prepared by Jesus for 3 ½ years. Their track record was not stellar to say the least. Peter had denied Christ three times and was still a little shaken from that dismal performance. Yet the grace and mercy of Our Heavenly Father sent forth HIS Holy Spirit to that house and empowered them from on High. And on that day, three thousand souls were added to their number and baptized. We too must prepare ourselves for that day when we thrust into the fullness. Yes, in one day your destiny can be fulfilled.

Power is given to the overcomer for the purpose of helping people. Jesus, our primary example, did not use His power to exploit people or make the Top 100 Wealthiest People list. Instead, "Jesus of Nazareth with the Holy Ghost and with power: who went about doing good, and healing all that were oppressed of the devil; for God was with him." There are those who have been given a measure of power but forgot the source of that power. Their ego began convincing them that they achieved the power on their own. In a subtle way, they exalt themselves over Our Heavenly Father. In Deuteronomy 8, we are given this warning:

> 17 "then you say in your heart, 'My power and the might of my hand have gained me this wealth.'
> 18 "And you shall remember the LORD your God, for it is He who gives you power to get wealth, *that He may establish His covenant* which He swore to your fathers, as it is this day.

Joseph's training required extreme trials in order that he would remember the depths a man can be placed being subject to Our Heavenly Father's judgment and will. Humbleness is a quality found in those who ascend to their calling by Love.

> James 4:10 Humble yourselves in the sight of the Lord, and he shall lift you up

> 1 Peter 5:5 … Yes, all of you be submissive to one another, and be clothed with humility, for "God resists the proud, But gives grace to the humble."
> 6 Therefore humble yourselves under the mighty hand of God, that He may exalt you in due time,

In the ascent, prosperity required for your calling will arrive and you can be sure that testing will ensue. Blessing is not primarily for consumption but arrives in order that you can and will bless others. One of the most critical aspects of stewardship is to hear Our Heavenly Father as HE directs you to give and not judge the recipient of the blessing. HE will have you give to people who seem undeserving, in sin, bitter, poor stewards, and a host of other apparent stumblingblocks. Your job is to obey the Word of THE LORD. If the other person did not have issues they were dealing with, they would not need to be blessed through you. As we diligently follow the directives from Heaven, our ascent into the fullness is unrestrained.

Our promotion from each test will require forgiveness. We can be assured that people will be used to test our commitment to our calling. Our ego needs an enemy and there are plenty of people out there willing to accommodate the situation. Their egos need someone to blame for their failures and you may be the selected target. As they see you being blessed, they will try to pull you down to their level for "misery loves company". When Jesus told the disciples in Matthew 18 they must forgive a brother 490 times, He was speaking of giving them a jubilee, releasing with complete forgiveness. We all long for a quiet and peaceful life but that is not going to happen as we go through the various stages of preparation.

> Matthew 6:12 And forgive us our debts, as we forgive our debtors. (KJV)

The word "as" means in the same way. Do unto others "as" you would have them do unto you. You must forgive in an unqualified manner if you want to be forgiven without condition. The wrongdoers must receive a full pardon from you for your ascent to be unrestrained. Live in the "now", not in the past. How long must we hold a grudge? Any punishment deserved by the other person will be administered by Our Heavenly Father:

> Romans 12:19 Dearly beloved, avenge not yourselves, but [rather] give place unto wrath: for it is written, Vengeance is mine; I will repay, saith the Lord. (KJV)

Freely you have received, freely give! As far as the east is from the west, so far hath he removed our transgressions from us! Forgiveness is required at each level of testing. Joseph had to forgive his brothers, his captors, Potiphar's wife, untold prisoners… Do you really think all those fellow prisoners were nice guys? Joseph was surely given the opportunity to forgive on a daily basis. His ascent was propelled by his understanding that Our Heavenly Father had a specific purpose for all of his trials and tribulation. That purpose required maturity, forgiveness, submission to authority, enduring setbacks, and descending into the depths of despair. Upon his identity being revealed to his brothers in Genesis 45, he reveals the understanding of "GOD sent me" three times:

5 Now therefore be not grieved, nor angry with yourselves, that ye sold me hither: for *God did send me* before you to preserve life.

7 And *God sent me* before you to preserve you a posterity in the earth, and to save your lives by a great deliverance.
8 So now *it was not you that sent me hither, but God:* and he hath made me a father to Pharaoh, and lord of all his house, and a ruler throughout all the land of Egypt. (KJV)

You must believe that you have a purpose for Our Heavenly Father is purposeful. HE created each of us with a specific purpose and with the gifts to fulfill that purpose. Those gifts must be developed, tried, and tested just like fine gold is refined. No matter what your current state, it is subject to change. All of Heaven is prepared to support your ascent in Love to the fulfillment of your calling. Jesus Christ paved the way for unfettered assistance needed to attain the fullness of your purpose. Your calling is like a magnet forever drawing you in its direction if only you will not resist. Your ego will attempt to thwart each step upward but you will learn to identify its motives and overcome its temptations. You will then look forward to serving mankind and be part of the flow of the Holy Spirit into bringing forth the Kingdom of GOD to earth as it is in Heaven!

Personal Assessment:
1. Write down the trials you have experience and see if you can determine why you went through them.
2. How are you different now than before your last major trial?
3. Are you mad at the person or persons who were instruments of your trial?
4. Did your trials produce unforgiveness or gratitude?
5. Are you an abuser of power and authority?

Chapter 14
THE FORGIVENESS OF LOVE

> "And forgive us our sins, just as we have forgiven those who have sinned against us."

Jesus shared with us a very simple and powerful prayer. Within this prayer are powerful truths that demand a greater understanding. Unforgiveness is a prevailing tool of the ego. When you have been wronged, your ego demands retribution and retaliation and you begin to plot ways to get back at that self-centered, thoughtless, arrogant... Oops! Now who are we talking about?

Isn't it true that we want everyone to treat us just like Jesus would have treated us? The ego wants the freedom to act in any fashion, usually in self-interest, but everyone else must act like a saint towards us. But Jesus in the above verse of Matthew 6:12 places a key word in the middle of the sentence- "as". That word is conditional in nature. This the above verse of the Lord's Prayer ties directly to:

> Matthew 7:2 "For with what judgment you judge, you will be judged; and with the measure you use, it will be measured back to you." (NKJV)

Both of these Scriptures refer to the Law of Attraction. Love attracts love and its associated attributes whereas unforgiveness attracts hate, division, contempt, discord, etc. What would you prefer to attract? This law is not reduced in any way by ignorance just as the law of gravity works the same for everyone, no exceptions. This Law of Attraction is a spiritual law and will operate at all levels, down to the physical. If this were not such an important law, Jesus would not have included it in the Lord's Prayer which is the standard of all prayers. If you sow seeds of unforgiveness, you will not be forgiven. If you sow seeds of strife and contention, you will live in strife and contention.

> Luke 6:38 "Give, and it will be given to you: good measure, pressed down, shaken together, and running over will be put into your bosom. For with the same measure that you use, it will be measured back to you." (NKJV)

This is one of the favorite Scriptures Christian use in the area of finances. Some throw it up to Heaven in an effort to force Our Heavenly Father to keep HIS Word as though HE needed to be reminded. Don't get me wrong, this Scripture is applicable to finances but it is all interwoven with the other areas of your life. Do you think that you can give money under this premise while you hate your brother and then expect to be blessed by Our Heavenly Father? Do you think that the Law of Attraction compartmentalizes your actions?

Does it seem like things are not going well for you? Could it be you are attracting various forms of judgment based on your past actions and attitude?

To reverse the judgment you have on yourself you must first ask Our Heavenly Father for forgiveness as stated in the Lord's Prayer. I suggest that you also ask Our Heavenly Father to bring to remembrance your acts that need special mention in your past. Have you abused relationships with others? Have you exploited individuals for gain? As HE brings each memory back to you, ask to be forgiven of that specific act. Clear the deck of all those failures to walk righteously. This is a cleansing process of the heart and soul. If there is a restitution to pay, pay it. If you don't have the means, ask Our Heavenly Father for help.

Secondly, you must forgive yourself. In order for this to happen, you must understand that Love created you and the Spirit of GOD is in you even though the Spirit may be "dormant". Your ego would have you believe otherwise. Your ego would have you believe that you are all alone and that Our Heavenly Father has forsaken you or dwells in some distant galaxy or you may believe that HE is an angry GOD just waiting for you to screw up again so that HE can get his big hammer out and bust you in the mouth. Both are wrong. HIS every action is based on the primary intent of Love. Your lack of awareness places scales over your eyes preventing you from seeing this reality. Reading this book will increase your awareness and comprehension of Our Heavenly Father's Love for you. Once this connection with Love is realized, there will be an outward manifestation that may surprise you at first. This Love has been buried deep in the recesses of your heart and it must be awakened to your consciousness. In the center of your heart is the purity of Love. It is the essence of who you are and is your primary "portal" to Our Heavenly Father. We are all connected to HIM thus HE can hear every prayer of every person HE created. But HE responds to righteousness. HE will answer prayer according to our pursuit of Love. Any ego-based prayer will not be acted upon based on the request but instead you may receive the opposite based on the need of furthering your education. To state another way, if you ask for something that promotes a path of sin, you will most likely receive a response that leads to correction. As you increase in awareness of Love within you, you will accept yourself as a child of GOD. You will further see the distinction of your true self versus the ego's attempt to convince you that you are some ogre than does not deserve forgiveness. You are Love!

"I don't deserve to be forgiven." Your ego will make any attempt to stay in control with thoughts like this. This statement tries to invalidate the Blood of Jesus Christ for it is His Blood that justifies us, not our own ability. Forgiveness of our lawlessness is a result of Love by Our Heavenly Father:

> Ephesians 2:
> 4 But God, who is rich in mercy, because of His great love with which He loved us,
> 5 even when we were dead in trespasses, made us alive together with Christ (by grace you have been saved),

6 and raised us up together, and made us sit together in the heavenly places in Christ Jesus,
7 that in the ages to come He might show the exceeding riches of His grace in His kindness toward us in Christ Jesus.
8 For by grace you have been saved through faith, and that not of yourselves; it is the gift of God,
9 not of works, lest anyone should boast. (NKJV)

As we embrace the Love of Our Heavenly Father, our soul conforms to the forgiving state of Love. The mind becomes a servant to our spirit of Love and the ego is subdued and restrained from ruling our every action. Love will then bring forth to remembrance those past actions and thoughts that need cleansing. As those memories surface, simply thank Our Heavenly Father for forgiving you of those acts and thoughts, and cleansing you of the unrighteousness. Remember this: if Our Heavenly Father, the Possessor of Heaven and earth, is willing to forgive you, how much more should you be willing to forgive yourself! Any thought of unworthiness originates from your ego attempting to keep you in bondage in order to prevent your calling from springing forth. You have the right as a child of the Most High GOD to fulfill your calling.

Thirdly, you must forgive others and you can be assured you will get the opportunity. In Luke 17 Jesus said, "Then He said to the disciples, "It is impossible that no offenses should come, but woe to him through whom they do come!" This is a very powerful statement. He says emphatically that we will be offended in some way, shape, or form thus we will all get the opportunity to forgive. We can have the greatest of intentions to live peaceably among all men but that will not eliminate the offenses. There are just some people looking for a fight. They have some deep seated issue that rules their life and they do not know how to resolve it and so they express their frustrations in an outward fashion, often in rage and bitterness. The Law of attraction accommodates them and they spiral downward towards ultimate physical destruction.

In the second verse, Jesus adds, "It would be better for him if a millstone were hung around his neck, and he were thrown into the sea, than that he should offend one of these little ones." Offending a follower of Christ is especially dangerous to your future. When Our Heavenly Father says "Vengeance is Mine", that is exactly what HE means. You need not worry about balancing the books with the offender. He will have the opportunity to go through the cleansing process possibly with extreme prejudice. Over the years, I have seen this play out time after time in my own life. I have been wronged by an offender and then later that person is a recipient of judgment. I am sure the question arises "Why is this happening to me?" when judgment arrives. This is a very important reason to forgive those who offend you. Love does not want the full weight of the Law to prevail over the offender. Love is always optimistic that the offender will be restored.

Jesus warns us to be on guard. If our brother sins against us, sternly warn him. You must put him on notice that he is being lawless so that there is no question of the breach that has arisen. Love created this universe with unlimited power and authority to compress and expand with such explosive power that one cannot fathom the energy it took to form the universes. Love isn't some dormant, passive state that is run over by a bully. Love confronts the offender, not to destroy but to restore. Destruction is the choice of the offender, not the offended. What if you are not sure about who is the offender in a situation? Look at the fruit, it will testify of the reality set before you.

Love demands release of the offender from the offense. If the offender repents, you must forgive him as a child of Love. If you are unwilling to forgive, you will attract judgment on yourself. You see, these offenders in your life act as a mirror into your soul. When you look into their eyes, do you see yourself? Jesus made a critical point of embracing this aspect of forgiveness. When asked how much forgiveness was to be offered, He said, "up to seventy times seven" or four hundred ninety times in one day, the number of jubilee! Jubilee is all about the release from debt and servitude. In this case, the offender is being released from impending judgment and being given the opportunity to no longer serve the ego.

The Apostle Paul knew the need of forgiveness more than most for his merciless persecution of Christians was well known. He knew that if Jesus Christ would forgive him, the Word of GOD must be true. By the Spirit he wrote in Colossians 3:

> 12 Therefore, as the elect of God, holy and beloved, put on tender mercies, kindness, humility, meekness, longsuffering; (NKJV)

Are you the "elect"? I would suggest you are since you are pursuing the character of THE MOST HIGH GOD. Those who reject HIS Love will be subject to the corrective judgment required to expose their lawlessness. This will only occur after much longsuffering. As we walk in a constant state of forgiveness, we will be clothed with a heart of tender mercies. We will also gain an appreciation for all life on earth. We will be kind to animals and plant life for they are also able to communicate to Our Heavenly Father. Science is now discovering how plants can respond to their owners, independent of distance or proximity of the owners to the plants. The plants respond to the intent of their owners. The fig tree was the recipient of such intent.

We will walk in humility because we have commanded our mind and body to become servants rather than control our every move. No longer will we act arrogant and entitled as though the universe revolved around our every move. Our extravagance will be replaced by moderation in all things. As our own walk conforms to Christ, then we act toward others as Jesus acts toward us:

> 13 bearing with one another, and forgiving one another, if anyone has a complaint against another; even as Christ forgave you, so you also must do.

The Beatitudes were a simple and direct set of truths that we all have the capacity to understand and walk by. As mentioned earlier, we attract the very thing that we project. Jesus said it like this:

"Blessed are the merciful, for they will receive mercy."

As we practice and extend mercy, we will attract mercy unto ourselves. As we are forebearing, longsuffering, patient, and kind, those very responses will be given to us as we walk in our own humanity. We must extend forgiveness daily and you can be assured that you will get the opportunity to practice. This goes against our intellect which constantly wants to judge the other person and "reconcile" the books. Remember, our mind judges everyone else by their actions but ourselves by our intent. As we practice forgiveness, we train our mind to be a servant, not our lord. When we practice forgiveness, our heart grows stronger and our character matures and grows closer to Our Heavenly Father's character. Our spirit gains clarity about the intent behind the acts of others. We see beyond the masquerade that is placed before us and can minister to the source of the issue, not the symptom. The power over us by others is removed for they can no longer manipulate us by feeding our ego. Their manipulation will now be met with revelation rather than blind subservience.

"Blessed are the pure in heart, for they will see God."

What a powerful statement! Think about it. Jesus made a claim that few can truly comprehend. As we practice mercy and forgiveness, we cleanse ourselves of unrighteousness. As our Love grows and we become more like Our Heavenly Father, we will see HIM in everything for HIS fingerprint is found in all of creation. Mercy and forgiveness promotes purity in the heart and purity of heart brings you into the presence of Our Heavenly Father. Our Heavenly Father is in the restoration business and this is the same business we must be in.

Personal Assessment:
1. Do you have unforgiveness in your heart for anybody, past or present?
2. Does someone need to forgive you?
3. Do you feel like you need to demand restitution for a wrong done to you?
4. Have you identified those thoughts and actions that are generated by your ego?
5. Go find someone who you have wronged and ask for their forgiveness.

Chapter 15

The Miracles of Love

John 14:12 "Most assuredly, I say to you, he who believes in Me, the works that I do he will do also; and greater works than these he will do, because I go to My Father. (NKJV)

Jesus spoke these parting words to His disciples before going to the Cross. He was emphatic about the expectation when He began the sentence with "most assuredly". We are to pay close attention to what Jesus is about to say. Though He is speaking to His disciples, this sentence is directed to he who believes, not just the immediate audience. The disciples had not been doing the works of Jesus as much as simply observing the works of Jesus. He had just explained to Thomas, "I am the way, and the truth, and the life". We are also to walk in "The Way". What is the "way"? It is the walk of Love!

Many Christians are satisfied to go about their daily lives without pursuing acts of Love. They believe that salvation was sufficient to assure their future and thus their life could go on as usual. Others wanted a little more than salvation and so they began to walk in faith. Many of them received the Baptism of The Holy Spirit and even operated in one of the Gifts of The Holy Spirit. They studied books on faith primarily to receive blessings of finance and health for them and their family. There is nothing wrong with expecting Our Heavenly Father to send health and finances your way, but there is still more.

Ask yourself this question: "Whom do I know personally, who does the same works of Jesus?" In the above Scripture, Jesus sets the standard for the person who walks in "The Way". This person will be fruitful just as Jesus was fruitful as illustrated by His works. He healed the sick, ministered to the broken-hearted, and preached the good news of the Love of Our Heavenly Father for all of mankind. There have been a few ministries around the world who have walked in this to some degree but by and large those ministries were the exception and not the rule. Some of the ministries were later plagued with scandal, often the result of money or sex motives.

Philip asked to see The Father and Jesus replied, "The person who has seen me has seen the Father!" The disciples were trying to comprehend Jesus' words. How could they do the same works as Jesus? Only if they could see The Father, Philip asked. Jesus told them that He explicitly had the same character as His Father. "If you have known me, you will know my Father too." Our most important focus should be to read, study, and comprehend the words and actions of Jesus if we want to do greater works. He was and is the manifested culmination of Love. His actions and words reflected the character of His Father. In order to truly understand the actions of a person, you must understand the intent behind those actions. In order to understand the intent, you must spend quality time with the person and begin to see what they say and how they respond to situations.

Obedience is the proof of genuine Love. If you love Me you will keep My commandments of Love. This is a never-ending circle. The commandments are based on Love and if you love Jesus you will keep those commandments. Yes, it is all about Love. Paul proclaimed himself to be a servant and apostle of Jesus Christ. He was sent by the One he served, not out of duty but out of Love. Paul realized that Jesus had saved him from certain death and destruction. The Love of Christ was greater than Paul's intention to kill Christians and he began to understand the grace and mercy of Our Heavenly Father. Previously he only understood the judgment of Our Heavenly Father as he was carrying out the Mosaic Law without understanding the character of Our Heavenly Father. When Paul met Jesus, he finally received the full understanding of the Law of Love. As we opt to choose grace over judgment when dealing with others, we too receive grace instead of judgment for our own sins. In cases where we are required to administer correction, our intent will be toward restoration rather

Ascending to Love

than division. As we obey the principles of Love, we open ourselves up to being used by Our Heavenly Father in the area of miracles and other works of Love. HE will use those people who reflect HIS character not some fleshly characteristic. Every miracle and good work is designed to bring people closer to Our Heavenly Father.

The first miracle of Jesus was to turn water into wine at the wedding in Cana. This first miracle was a clear indication that Jesus had command of "God" particles, the smallest particle of matter in the universe. HE was able to command particles to assimilate into a new resulting substance- wine. The symbology of this first miracle is important to understand in the mosaic of man's progression through time. The water was transformed into the Tabernacles offering of wine. During Tabernacles, the priest would pour out both water and wine as an offering to Our Heavenly Father. This transformation is indicative of the Sons of GOD being transformed as an offering of service to mankind and should occur before the fullness of the Tabernacles period. The Sons of GOD are set apart for the service of bringing forth the fullness of the revelation of Our Lord Jesus Christ. How do we know this represents the "Sons of GOD"? It is hidden within the amount of water using a little bit of mathematics and understanding the historic equivalent of a firkin.

Six waterpots X three firkins = 18 firkins total.
1 firkin = 8.5 Imperial gallons.
18 x 8.5 = 153 Imperial gallons.

Using American gallons: we know that the waterpots contained two or three firkins apiece thus the average is 2.5 firkins each. They were filled to the brim.

Six waterpots X 2.5 firkins - 15 firkins
1 firkin = 10.2 American gallons.
15 x 10.2 = 153 American gallons.

The following Hebrew expression for 'Sons of God' has a numeric value of exactly "153":

(Beth/Nun/Yud Heh/Aleph/Lamed/Chet/Yud/Mem)

These are the ones who will usher in the next age of revelation and consciousness. These are the ones who have and will press in to the understanding of the revelation of Love. They will be found worthy of stewardship by the fact that they know the character of Our Heavenly Father- Love. They will immerse themselves in Love until every aspect of their life has been baptized by this understanding. The Way is the way of Love and Jesus prepared the Way by providing us a perfect example of the way Love operates. The fruit of Love of the Sons of GOD will be compared to the fruit of Jesus. In order to lead the way into the Kingdom being established on earth, we must understand the Kingdom sufficiently. How do we go about obtaining this understanding?

> Ephesians 3: 17 that the Christ dwell in your hearts through faith in love, rooted and grounded,
> 18 so that ye be strong to apprehend with all the saints what the breadth and length and depth and height, 19 and to know the love of the Christ which passeth knowledge, that ye be filled unto all the fullness of God. (Panin Numeric New Testament)

How are we to walk in the fullness of Our Heavenly Father as Jesus did? We must be rooted and grounded in Love. Our faith in HIS Word propels us through this process of becoming rooted and grounded in Love. As we study HIS Word in the area of Love, we are planting those seeds in our fertile ground. As we continue to water those seeds they begin to grow in us. As we began to operate in the Word of Love, those seeds burst out into plants and roots began to establish themselves in our very essence. Day after day we are determined to access power hidden from mankind for eons. We are not deterred from our goal of producing the fruit of Love. This power has been reserved for those who would be faithful to the revelation and Character of Our Heavenly Father. Greed has no place near this revelation. The revelation would be protected from those who would attempt to pervert its use for their own personal gain. In the presence of Love, greed cannot exist as well as other sins. The cleansing of the Word of GOD prepares our soil for the planting of this agape Love.

> Ephesians 3:18 may be able to comprehend with all the saints what is the width and length and depth and height (NKJV)

The above passage mentions four dimensions: the width and length and depth and height. I believe the term "depth" here represents our fourth dimension of time. As we are rooted and grounded in Love, we will receive revelation of operating in the four dimensions. We will be able to command those particles just as Jesus was able to change water into wine and provide for the need at the time.

Knowledge is good but the Love of Christ surpasses knowledge. As we focus on Love, our understanding will rise above knowledge and we will tap into the fullness of Our Heavenly Father. No longer will miracles be sparse or incidental. No longer will our ministry produce a frustration from lack of manifested results. Mankind has been on a quest for knowledge yet with access to more knowledge through the Internet, man has ascended no higher than his computer keyboard. Wisdom and understanding from above are accessible as we comprehend the Love of Christ and manifest its fruits in our own lives.

This first miracle of Jesus at the wedding in Cana manifested His glory and the disciples believed on Him. The manifestation of the fruit of Love brings forth belief in the fullness of Our Heavenly Father. Faith can manifest the giftings of the Holy Spirit to a lesser degree. Our Heavenly Father's grace allows for that as we are in pursuit of Love. As our revelation of Love grows, our ability to bring forth the Glory as a testimony will be the witness of the veracity of this third baptism. The miracles wrought from Love will perplex those who have based their life on the pursuit of knowledge and will disintegrate the paradigm of their ego. The Gospel of John is known as the Gospel of Love. John was known as the beloved disciple and wrote from the perspective of Love. This miracle was the first of eight signs in the Gospel and foretells of the transformation of the "Sons of GOD" to manifest HIS glory.

Immediately after Jesus performed this first miracle, He dealt with the most subtle hindrance to Love, the love of money, or greed. He cleansed the temple of the moneychangers. The temple had slowly moved from a house of prayer to a house of merchandise. As we focus on Love, our "temple" will be cleansed of greed. The basis of greed is scarcity. If we have command over the resources of the earth, scarcity will no longer be an issue because the sustenance needed can be attained by the command of Love. As we focus our Love on fruit and vegetable plants, they should increase their production in response to our Love. As we express our gratitude for our food at the table, its intrinsic benefit to our body will increase and provide the fullness of nutrients locked inside of it. Gratitude is the key to the heart and praying over our food is an expression of that gratitude.

The second miracle (or sign) in the Gospel of John was the healing of the nobleman's son. Love has no issue with time or distance. Jesus had returned to Cana and the nobleman's son was in Capernaum. This miracle is a clear indication that the power unlocked by the revelation of Love transcends time and distance without issue. This miracle expands our understanding of Love not being limited by the four earthly dimensions but shows us that we can and will operate according to Heaven's dimensions.

Nathanael whose name means "Gift of GOD" was from Cana. He was described by Jesus as the man with no guile (or deceit). It is only appropriate that the first two prophetic signs in the Gospel of John would occur in the town where the man with no guile or deceit was found. These first signs are two witnesses of the genuine nature of the outworking of Love.

The third sign was the healing of the impotent man. This man had been incapacitated for thirty-eight years, the same amount of time the children of Israel had extended their stay in the wilderness. This was at the time of the winter feast, probably Purim. The Feast of Purim represented the deliverance of the Jews from the greed of Haman, found in the book of Esther. The man had a chronic infirmity that left him weak and he had clearly submitted to the reality that his infirmity was in control. However, Love supersedes the control of sickness and disease. Just as Jesus commanded the particles of water in the first sign, the sub-atomic particles that made up the impotent man's body responded to His command as well. The man's body was restored to its original design. Can you imagine the impact Love would have on the current healthcare system? As the revelation of Love manifests its fruits, the Heavenly economy will replace the current economy of greed. When the man was healed, he was able to fulfill his purpose. In the same sense, the children of Israel were able to enter the Promised Land after their affliction of unbelief was removed from their midst.

The fourth sign found in the Gospel was the feeding of the five thousand. The five barley loaves and the two fishes are both Tabernacles signs of those overcomers being "food" for the multitudes. The Kingdom economy operates in abundance rather than lack. The multiplication of the loaves and fishes was another indication of the ability of Love to meet the needs of the people as well as bless the provider of the food. Being in command of the physical requires us to be good stewards over the revelation. Can you imagine what would happen if greed entered into the equation? We would be left with five thousand hungry men! Greed would have withheld the loaves and fishes in fear of reprisal from the parent expecting the boy to return home with the food. Love sent home twelve baskets of food instead. Love saw no need to submit to the circumstances of lack and as we immerse ourselves in this revelation of Love, we should expect nothing less.

How many people have you heard of that can walk on water? This fifth sign defies human logic. We must remember that Jesus had not yet been resurrected from the dead thus He was operating in human flesh just as we are. His communion with Our Heavenly Father provided Him the necessary revelation and power to bring forth these signs. He is our example and we must grasp that reality. How can we do greater things if we don't? As you read the words of Jesus written in the four Gospels, you should now be able to see that His focus was on the revelation of Love. He revealed the character of our Heavenly Father in the Law by summarizing it into two commandments with Love being the cornerstone. "For GOD so Loved the world HE gave" is such a simple and powerful truth that has been hidden in the open. Jesus' own body submitted to the command of Love and defied the gravity which would have caused Him to sink in the water. You could use the excuse that since Jesus is the Son of GOD, He should have been able to walk on water. But what about Peter? Peter was also able to walk on water even though it was temporary. In the presence of Love, faith can defy the natural as well as the fear of failure. Faith without Love can produce temporary results but when both are present the fullness of The Father prevails. Within this sign is another phenomenon- teleportation. The boat was immediately on the other side of the sea after Jesus arrived on the scene. Does this mean that Love has an answer to the energy crisis as well?

Sign number six refers to the man who was born blind. As we come face to face with Love, our eyes will be opened and the revelation will be revealed. Men would have us remain in a blind state so they can control our lives. The truth will set you free from the lies that would enslave you. Sickness and disease are a multi-trillion dollar business and those who stand to gain are not interested in the population being healed and made whole by spiritual means. Who would then buy all the pharmaceuticals? What would happen to all the drug stores found on every corner in America? What would happen to the nursing homes if all the elderly lived healthy until the appointed day of physical passing? Ignorance is not bliss. In the Pentecostal age there have been many confirmed healings. The problem is that as a percentage of those wanting to be healed, the numbers are small. Why? The revelation of Love has been comprehended only in part. The man born blind is a type and shadow of our own state of blindness. As we pursue the character of Our Heavenly Father and walk in communion with Him just as Jesus did (and still does), we will

Ascending to Love

take on His Character of Love. Our blindness will be "healed" and we will be able to see clearly. The fruit will begin to manifest as we are moved with compassion for our fellow man. The church leaders at the time were upset that Jesus would heal on the Sabbath. Instead of gratitude for the restoration of man, they were critical of Jesus. Their egos wanted to maintain control of the masses by keeping them enslaved to their traditions. What a sad commentary! How many blind people do you know who would want to wait one more day to receive the precious gift of sight?

"Lord, look, the one you love is sick." The seventh sign occurred in Bethany, the place where Jesus liked to hang out. Lazarus clearly was dear to Jesus. His sisters sent a message to Jesus to compel Him to return to Bethany immediately. It was evident that they had faith in Jesus' ability to heal Lazarus. Instead of making haste in response to their request, Jesus tarried for two days. Now Jesus loved Martha and her sister and Lazarus so the lack of action had nothing to do with them. This sign was to show that even death must respond to Love. There is no aspect of man's life that is unresponsive to Love for Love has removed the sting of death. Once again those GOD particles responded to Love's command. Not only had Lazarus suffered sickness, he had died and was placed in the tomb. His body had already begun to decay for he "stinketh". The situation looked pretty bleak to the natural eye but Jesus said that Lazarus was merely sleeping, not in a permanent state of death. This seventh sign confirmed that Love's power and authority is greater than physical death and atrophy. Neither a withered hand, nor a cutoff ear, nor even death can resist Love's command. Jesus waited two days before proceeding from Jerusalem to Bethany. Could this be a type and shadow of the two thousand year Pentecostal reign before the fullness of Love would be revealed to mankind? If so, we should expect Love to permeate our spirit, soul and bodies to enable us to walk with this same power and authority. If we truly accept Jesus as our "older brother" and expect to do greater things, we must come to the realization that Love IS the path we must take in order to receive the necessary anointing to walk in this same state and produce even greater manifestations as Jesus prophesied.

We must embrace His prophecy as we focus on taking on the character of Our Heavenly Father so that we can truly say "My Father and I are one!"

The eighth and final sign in the Gospel of John was the catching of the 153 fish. This sign is the bookend to the first sign where Jesus turned the water into wine. In both cases there was lack due to insufficiency and Jesus revealed His glory. In the first sign, He revealed His glory while in the flesh whereas in the eight sign, He revealed His glory while in His glorified body. In this chapter, the disciples had been fishing all night and throwing their nets off the left side of the boat, left representing judgment. When morning came (or the new day), Jesus appeared unto them but they did not recognize Him. From the shore, He told them to cast their net off the right side of the boat, the right side denoting mercy. This time they caught 153 great fish AND the net did not break. In the other story of catching fish, the net broke. The Sons of GOD are called to feed the world with the Word of GOD. Where else would you find the details of this prophetic sign other than the Gospel of John, the beloved disciple? John had the revelation of Love and wrote from this perspective. He wrote again in 1 John 3:

> 1 Behold, what manner of love the Father hath bestowed upon us, that we should be called the sons of God: therefore the world knoweth us not, because it knew him not.
> 2 Beloved, now are we the sons of God, and it doth not yet appear what we shall be: but we know that, when he shall appear, we shall be like him; for we shall see him as he is. (KJV)

The Sons of GOD are called to be instruments of mercy for a world who does not understand the Love of GOD. As this chapter continues "This is now the third time that Jesus shewed himself to his disciples, after that he was risen from the dead". Jesus presented Himself for the third time, letting everything be established by two or three witnesses. As Jesus and the disciples were eating the fish, Jesus spoke to Peter in John 21:

Ascending to Love

> 15 So when they had dined, Jesus saith to Simon Peter, Simon, [son] of Jonas, lovest (agapao) thou me more than these? He saith unto him, Yea, Lord; thou knowest that I love (phileo) thee. He saith unto him, Feed my lambs.

Shouldn't this be sufficient to convince Peter of the mission? Jesus just appeared in His resurrected body and I would expect that the disciples were paying close attention to every word Jesus spoke. But Jesus continued:

> 16 He saith to him again the second time, Simon, [son] of Jonas, lovest (agapao) thou me? He saith unto him, Yea, Lord; thou knowest that I love (phileo) thee. He saith unto him, Feed my sheep.

Once again the emphasis is on Love, not anything else. As if twice wasn't enough, Jesus speaks again:

> 17 He saith unto him the third time, Simon, [son] of Jonas, lovest thou me? Peter was grieved because he said unto him the third time, Lovest (phileo) thou me? And he said unto him, Lord, thou knowest all things; thou knowest that I love (phileo) thee. Jesus saith unto him, Feed my sheep. (KJV)

The Greek word "phileo" denotes a conditional Love whereas "agapao" is unconditional Love. Peter was not yet ready to move from conditional Love to unconditional Love. That would soon change with the arrival of the Baptism of the Holy Spirit. Peter would soon find out the all mankind would be the focus of Love, not just the Jewish nation. All men have been wandering in blindness to Our Heavenly Father's Love. Jesus performed miracles on behalf of all mankind for He did not discriminate against those who were oppressing the Jews. He made this clear to Paul and Peter either by vision or direct encounter. The Gentiles were to receive the Gospel as well.

Each of the eight signs in John was an impartation of Love. Jesus summarized the Law with Love. His third appearance after His resurrection was centered around Love. The essence of His entire ministry was because "GOD so loved the world". The Sons of GOD will reflect this same character as they are empowered with the revelation of Love and the resulting fruit. Greater miracles will be manifested under this anointing. This is the Tabernacles anointing that will be the fullness of Our Heavenly Father. Love will expose the hearts of men and they will come to repentance. The miracles will precede the Sons of GOD as they are "fed" to the people to usher in the Kingdom. Finally, the cry for the Kingdom to come will be brought forth and Love will be "The Way".

Personal Assessment:
1. Have you personally experienced a miracle directly attributed to Our Heavenly Father?
2. Study the miracles of Jesus and the disciples.
3. Find a book on Smith Wigglesworth and read of the miracles of his ministry.
4. Find a book on the ministry of T.L. Osborn and read of the miracles of his ministry.
5. Ask Our Heavenly Father to use you in the expression of miracles in other peoples' lives.

Chapter 16
The Peace of Love

"Glory to God in the highest, And on earth peace among men with whom He is pleased."

Peace can be elusive whether be on an individual level or national level. Each of us seeks peace in our inner soul and we simply want to be in balance with the universe. When we wake up in the morning after a peaceful night's sleep, we want to look forward to another day of gratitude to Our Heavenly Father for placing us on this earth. None of us want to wake up behind a dumpster wondering where our next meal will come from nor do we want to go to bed hungry and cold. Did Our Heavenly Father put us on this earth with an insufficiency of natural resources to sustain us? I think not.

Abraham was called to be the "Father of many nations". At the time of making this covenant, Our Heavenly Father said in Genesis 15:15, "And thou shalt go to thy fathers in peace; thou shalt be buried in a good old age." Isn't that the goal of all of us, to live a peaceful, long life? How can we attain this goal? Only by ascending to Love!

Psalm 119:165 Great peace have they which love thy law: and nothing shall offend them. (KJV)

As we Love the Law and the Lawgiver, peace will come to us even though war is raging all around us. As we seek to be lawful, we eliminate the need to protect our lawlessness. Let me explain. I once worked for a man who wrote down everything he said in a meeting, phone call, or any other form of communication. On the other hand I had a simple way of remembering by asking the question: What is the truth? That was my position. I didn't need to write down what I told people, I simply needed to recall the truth of the situation. People who constantly exceed the speed limit have to expend extra energy in their attempt to evade their adversary. Their lawlessness promotes anxiety whereas if they would only drive the speed limit, they could enjoy the journey. Is saving a few minutes here and there worth promoting lawlessness in your life?

Paul understood how peace and Love worked together when he penned the following to the church at Corinth, "Finally, brethren, farewell. Become complete. Be of good comfort, be of one mind, live in peace; and the God of love and peace will be with you".

Our Heavenly Father is the author of Love and peace. Do you think there is turmoil in the Throne Room of Heaven? HE placed the planets and the stars in perfect equilibrium, created the smallest particles to respond in peace toward each other to produce atoms, molecules, elements, substances, plants, and animals.

Man's ego would upset this equilibrium by pursuing greed and self interest rather than living in peace toward others. The ego would have us believe that scarcity is the prevailing law while he fails to look around at all of the resources available. The ego seeks to create a problem so that it can solve it and exalt itself above others. The ego is the source of this internal conflict that causes peace to be so elusive to us on an individual basis. As our egos band together we produce a society with an attitude of entitlement. Our egos promote an air of adversity that causes us to sleep with one eye open for fear that the next person will steal from us. Those of us that seek to live in peace in the midst of a society like this are tested daily. As we take on the character of Our Heavenly Father we are no longer moved by the lawlessness that surrounds us. No, we don't deny its existence but we simply don't let it steal our peace. This life of Love produces good fruit and Paul expounded on this fruit in Galatians chapter 5:

22 But the fruit of the Spirit is love, joy, peace, longsuffering, kindness, goodness, faithfulness,

23 gentleness, self-control. Against such there is no law. (NKJV)

I believe the fruit is listed in a specific order to show first and foremost you must have Love before the other fruit can and will fully manifest. Certainly when you are walking in Love your joy will be fulfilled and when a person has both Love and joy, they will have peace that passeth all understanding. Other men will wonder how you are able to have peace when the circumstances would dictate otherwise. Once we fully embrace Love, we will walk in peace even among the tests and trials of life on this earth.

"May mercy and peace and love be multiplied to you." Jude expressed the reality that peace can grow and be multiplied in each of us. All of us have experienced no peace, a little peace, and some of us great peace. In times of great turmoil, our peace comes when we realize that Our Heavenly Father has not forsaken us but HIS Love keeps us through it all. The revelation that we have eternal life after physical death is peaceful within itself. Comprehension of eternity and infinite provides peace when set against a backdrop of the Love of Jesus Christ who died for us out of Love for us.

When I was young, I knew my parents would protect me and Love me no matter what I did. How much more does My Heavenly Father Love me as well. This assurance brings forth peace and comfort in the midst of fiery trials. Our Heavenly Father is quick to provide us with what we need in times of distress. His Most Holy Spirit is given for our benefit:

> Luke 11:11 If a son shall ask bread of any of you that is a father, will he give him a stone? or if [he ask] a fish, will he for a fish give him a serpent?
> 12 Or if he shall ask an egg, will he offer him a scorpion?
> 13 If ye then, being evil, know how to give good gifts unto your children: how much more shall [your] heavenly Father give the Holy Spirit to them that ask him? (KJV)

When we ask and receive the Holy Spirit into our lives we receive peace in our souls. We come to the realization of the intimacy that

Our Heavenly Father wants to share with us. No longer is HE a distant God but now a Father. HE Loves me specifically and personally. You too! As we pursue Love, peace will follow. Our faith will be empowered knowing that HE has our best interest at heart. As we quiet our souls, we will sense HIS leading in our lives. We will sense favor among men turning toward us rather than remaining elusive as it has in the past. Our peace will precede us as we enter into a situation and division and turmoil will dissipate. Fruitfulness will abound toward our account and doors of opportunity will open up, all promoting peace in our lives. As we get older, we can age gracefully. Our health improves as our physiology responds to the peace that we walk in. Peace moves our body from the acidic to the alkaline state thus providing no fuel for cancer to grow. Our cells are no longer in rebellion but respond to the messages sent to them by our spirit. Our outlook becomes contagious to others who are desperately seeking what we have. The vacuum in their souls is like a radar attempting to detect that missing ingredient though it is hidden in plain sight.

The Holy Spirit is our advocate in the Divine Court. When our accusers attempt to rob our peace from us by lobbing salvos of false or misleading accusations, our Advocate represents our best interest in this Divine Court. There is such a peace knowing that when the lawless accusations come, the verdict will be returned in favor of Love and peace for our judge is The Righteous One, not some man or woman whose bias could evoke an unrighteous response. There is peace just knowing that the Holy Spirit is at all times ready to represent our best interest. What if we are guilty? We know that the mercy of Our Heavenly Father will sustain us through whatever righteous judgment is warranted. HE will use this judgment as an opportunity to teach us HIS ways even though our flesh would prefer other methods of learning.

What about times of great turmoil and anxiety? Our Heavenly Father has got that covered too. HE created angels as our ministering spirits to be dispatched during our time of need:

> Daniel 10:10 Suddenly, a hand touched me, which made me tremble on my knees and on the palms of my hands.
> 11 And he said to me, "O Daniel, man greatly beloved, understand the words that I speak to you, and stand upright, for I have now been sent to you." While he was speaking this word to me, I stood trembling. (NKJV)

Angels are dispatched as the need arises. Generally, they are not seen by the human eye but nonetheless they are acting on our behalf. As we pray according to the Will of Our Heavenly Father, our prayers will be answered. Depending on the need, those prayers may necessitate the dispatching of one or more angels on our behalf. Our calling may require intervention in the Heavenlies just as Daniel's calling needed angelic intervention. As we understand the reality and purpose of angels, our peace is strengthened. Our Heavenly Father has sufficient resources available for every need that may arise. As we navigate through this life, we can be assured that there is no challenge that cannot be met and overcome. That assurance promotes peace in our lives.

Once we are walking in Love and peace, our sphere of influence increases. Our household begins to change. Our Love overcomes the obstacles of others who would prefer us to live in the same turmoil they are experiencing. Have you ever noticed that misery loves company? Their ego needs to justify their misery by ruining your day if possible. It seems as though their goal is simply to steal your peace and they will do anything they can to achieve that end result. As our Love matures, our peace cannot be stolen for we now are able to see the devices that person uses in their attempts to challenge you. Before long it becomes somewhat amusing to see their attempts to control you. It is like watching a child attempting to manipulate you. Your eyes have been opened to their ego's attempt to control you. Once that occurs, the battle is won and you are no longer a pawn of their troubled soul. Instead you become a light and expose their turmoil. This exposure gives them the opportunity to embrace the Love of Our Heavenly Father and change. Love stands its ground and peace provides that double witness that is needed when being challenged by another. Our walk begins to affect others in our household and promotes peace in those relationships. Love begins to command the decisions and direction of the family. No longer are members of the family demanding their own way but are willing to defer to others and the family becomes unified. Others see the transformation and begin to inquire. This provides a basis by which we can testify of the Love of Our Heavenly Father.

As peace becomes an integral part of our daily life, decisions improve. No longer are our decisions tainted by the turmoil that has been plaguing us. Our decisions tend to be based on long range benefits rather than the immediate and temporary satisfaction. We are now willing to sacrifice the immediate and temporary benefit for the sustainable, longer term. This is a sign of wisdom from above. James tell us in chapter 3, verse 17:

> "But the wisdom that is from above is first pure, then peaceable, gentle, willing to yield, full of mercy and good fruits, without partiality and without hypocrisy."

Wisdom and peace go hand in hand. I have noticed that I have become gentle as I have grown in the revelation of Love. Sports encourage competition and the "take no prisoners" attitude. Without restraint, the competitive spirit will define a person's life. They will live and die by the performance of their team. This competiveness promotes division, "you are either for us or against us". The professional sports industry has exploited the ego's need to control. Fans like to see the opposing team's best player taken out of the game by injury for they must win at all cost. When a person's day is ruined by their favorite team's failure, it is clear that they do not walk in the peace that passeth understanding. I have noticed that I no longer have the strong desire to watch professional sports though I was once an avid fan. I now can enjoy a sporting event without it defining the rest of my day. That is good fruit!

When one is peaceful, he or she is willing to yield to another's preferences as long as there is no lawlessness promoted. No longer is there a mandate of "my way or the highway". Sacrifice of self is not an issue anymore. Love is more interested in furthering the relationship and fellowship than having temporary satisfaction tied to an event. As you mature in this walk, the desires of your heart are satisfied by a Loving Heavenly Father. Doors open that promote the path of your calling.

Wisdom brings forth good fruit by attraction rather than force. As we walk in Love, peace, and wisdom people and resources are attracted to us. This is a universal law. Jesus attracted GOD particles to feed the five thousand. One hundred fifty-three fish were attracted to the net. A fish with a coin in its mouth was attracted to be caught and provide Caesar his tribute. The ego lives in a force-based economy whereas Love brings forth an attraction-based economy. Men were drawn by the Holy Spirit rather than herded like cattle. Christians are likened to sheep and fish who easily and simply accept others. Sheep are led by the Shepherd not forced in a direction. We once had a few sheep to keep grass manageable on a small acreage. When I would try to catch one of them, I would chase the animal until it gave up and dropped to the ground. At that point it would go nowhere. You cannot easily herd sheep.

Peace cannot be purchased. Jesus spoke of the potential snare of wealth in the following parable in Luke 12:

> 16 Then He spoke a parable to them, saying: "The ground of a certain rich man yielded plentifully.
> 17 And he thought within himself, saying, 'What shall I do, since I have no room to store my crops?'
> 18 So he said, 'I will do this: I will pull down my barns and build greater, and there I will store all my crops and my goods.
> 19 And I will say to my soul, "Soul, you have many goods laid up for many years; take your ease; eat, drink, and be merry."'
> 20 But God said to him, 'Fool! This night your soul will be required of you; then whose will those things be which you have provided?'
> 21 "So is he who lays up treasure for himself, and is not rich

toward God." (NKJV)

Someone poor can have more peace than the wealthiest of men, and they most often do. Wealth has its subtle deceptions attached to it and I am convinced that unless you have a calling to handle wealth as a vessel of honor, you will have great difficulty in achieving peace from Above. Evil creeps in as men gain wealth. They transfer their trust from Heaven to their bank account. Once they have enough money to effectively retire their lack of peace drives them to gain more wealth, thinking that more wealth will bring the peace that is missing in their soul. They often attempt to fill the void with "things" or alcohol but nothing works. They have forgotten that peace originates from Our Heavenly Father and the trust that comes with that relationship must be greater than their wealth. Men lose sight that their physical walk is only a small aspect of eternity and when they die, all their wealth will stay here. In the meantime, their wealth could have been a blessing to the poor, the widows, and the orphans. When you are given the gift of producing wealth, it is not given for you to hoard but it is given for you to be a blessing to others. As Love prevails, the money flows. This is why it is called a medium of exchange. Just as blood flows through the body, money is to flow through the economy to maintain a healthy state. When we respond in Love to give to others, peace flows in our life. Who in their right mind would want to be called a "Fool" by Our Heavenly Father?

Fear is everywhere in today's world. The lawlessness among the people has grown to the point where the average person must be on guard at all times. When I was growing up, we slept with our front door open to let the cool night air flow through the house. Yes, the screen door was locked but it certainly would not keep out any intruders. Nowadays, everyone keeps their house locked most of the time. Home invasions are on the rise. The fear created by the lawless is best overcome by peace from Above. The lawless must not determine our peace but we must let Love prevail and guide us through the opportunities to be fearful. We must trust that "still small voice" to lead us down the proper path, moving us away from evil and lawlessness. We must look at delays as ordained from Our Heavenly Father

Ascending to Love

to prevent us from some adverse situation. As we walk in Love, peace will prevail in fearful situations.

> Luke 12:32 Fear not, little flock; for it is your Father's good pleasure to give you the kingdom. (KJV)

Be assured that Our Heavenly Father has our best interest at heart. HE will not guide you into fear, loss, and death but has your best interest at heart. It IS HIS pleasure to give us the Kingdom!

As we walk in the revelation of Love, peace abounds in our lives and we sow peace in others as well. Our words and actions eliminate contention and division. Those who are looking for a fight are disappointed and convicted of their actions. Their ego loses control of the situation and their unrighteousness is exposed. James shares this reality in the following passage:

> James 3:18 And the fruit of righteousness is sown in peace of them that make peace. (KJV)

In the Sermon on the Mount, Jesus expounds concise and impacting truths for all mankind to ponder and respond accordingly. Those who are following peace in this Love walk will be known as peacemakers and what will Heaven call them? Out of Jesus' own mouth:

> Matthew 5:9 Blessed are the peacemakers, For they shall be called sons of God. (NKJV)

What a privilege to be known as one of the "sons of God"! What could be a greater honor than to serve the Most High GOD! As we take on HIS character of Love and produce the fruit of righteousness, we put into motion ever-increasing peace. Yes, peace can be multiplied and that is good news. Peace begets peace. Peter understood this as he writes in one of his epistles:

2 Peter 1:
2 Grace and peace be multiplied to you in the knowledge of God and of Jesus our Lord,
3 as His divine power has given to us all things that pertain to life and godliness, through the knowledge of Him who called us by glory and virtue,
4 by which have been given to us exceedingly great and precious promises, that through these you may be partakers of the divine nature, having escaped the corruption that is in the world through lust. (NKJV)

As we pursue the attributes of Our Heavenly Father, expressed in His Most Holy Son, and empowered by His Most Holy Spirit, we will be partakers of the divine nature for HE has given to us exceedingly great and precious promises. As you continue to focus on the greatest revelation to be given to mankind, you will join me on the path less traveled. This path is called "The Way". Man's ego will do anything and everything to cause us to detour toward the path of death and destruction. Men on that path will purse control and exploitation of mankind. Money and power are their gods. Their day of reckoning will arrive soon enough. But all their power and resources is no match for the revelation of Love. This revelation will bring forth the Kingdom of GOD on earth where other secondary revelations have failed. Those with this revelation will be entrusted with the Keys of the Kingdom. The resources of the universe will be at their beck and call. The transfer of wealth will be placed into the hands of those not moved by its appeal but will treat money as a commodity rather than an instrument of control. The secrets of darkness will be revealed by those who will walk uprightly and fulfill the righteous judgment of Our Heavenly Father. Just as Jesus ascended on the third day and replaced his "woolens" with linen, so will we ascend to the Love of our Heavenly Father!

Personal Assessment:
1. Are you at peace? If not, why?
2. Do you promote peace among your co-workers, friends, and loved ones?
3. Do you constantly complain?
4. Do you promote gossip and half-truths?
5. Do your actions and/or words belittle others?

Chapter 17
THE CHOICE OF LOVE

Any parent who has eagerly awaited their child to embrace the concept of Love and express it understands free will. If your loved one says "I love you" only because it is expected or demanded then you really do not have an expression of Love. Love chooses to express itself in a willingness to be a blessing to the other person. Some would have us believe free will does not exist because of the sovereignty of GOD. They demand an "either, or" answer but I believe the reality to be that both free will and sovereignty are alive and well in the universe. Love demands free will. The ego demands no choice to serve others because it desperately wants to keep you in the shackles of its control.

> Joshua 24:14 "Now therefore, fear the LORD, serve Him in sincerity and in truth, and put away the gods which your fathers served on the other side of the River and in Egypt. Serve the LORD!
> 15 And if it seems evil to you to serve the LORD, choose for yourselves this day whom you will serve, whether the gods which your fathers served that were on the other side of the River, or the gods of the Amorites, in whose land you dwell. But as for me and my house, we will serve the LORD." (NKJV)

"Choose ye this day" is a common question posed in Scripture. If there were no choice there would be no question posed. A Loving Father would grant us free will to make a choice of Love versus lust. As a parent, Our Heavenly Father wants us to choose life by our own unfettered desire to serve Him. That is the ultimate expression of Love. Our Heavenly Father did not create a world of robots to simply carry out a complex game for Him to interact with. On the contrary, HE created man to mature into sons and daughters to experience creation and enjoy it in fellowship. In order to appreciate the good, we must experience the bad. Without the bad, how could we express our gratitude for being delivered from it?

Rest is more enjoyable after you have toiled outside in the yard. A cool drink tastes better after being in the scorching heat. Life is full of comparisons that provide us with appreciation and gratitude. We will experience hardships in life and those events are to be remembered when we receive our deliverance from them. We are not to dwell on them as though they are the reason for our existence but to use them as points of deliverance. We must not let our hope be deferred but let it be our expectation in those challenges we face. Even when Joseph was in the pit, he knew his calling was given by the Most High GOD and that somehow, some way, he would survive what appeared to be imminent death. We must never lose sight of where we have been but we must not continue living there in our minds. We must live in the "now".

Serving Our Heavenly Father is a choice when we submit to the leading of the Holy Spirit. A man who was in debt to another was required to become a servant until the debt was paid. However once the debt was paid, the servant could continue serving his master. He was then known as a bondservant for he now served out of Love rather than duty. It was his choice. A servant is devoted to another to the disregard of one's own interests. However, if the one you are devoted to has your best interest at heart, it is a win-win situation. Who better than the Creator of Heaven and earth to be the one you are devoted to! When you place your life in another man's hands, you are restricted to his views, interests, and resources. If necessary, that man would throw you under the bus if adversities arose that challenged his capacity to handle them. But Our Heavenly Father has no limitation so why would we refrain from serving Him? I can only conclude that the lack of revelation would keep us from making that choice.

Our choices will be tested for if there was no test, how committed are we to our choice? How many of us have decided to follow The LORD only to see that the decision was immediately challenged by an alternative? You can almost guarantee the test to come quickly. Just as we test the reliability of structures we build, our faith in the decision to follow Christ will be tested. Some tests are small and easy to overcome but others will test us to our very soul. Those tests may require a miracle on our behalf but Our Heavenly Father will be there at every turn. Our adversaries may appear to have certain victory but Heaven's resources will ultimately prevail as we submit our challenges to Our Heavenly Father, for HE knows the beginning from the end. Our choices are often tested and our commitment to those choices are measured in the midst of the tests.

Paul gives us instructions in the third chapter of Colossians. He urges us to "put on" and "let":

> 12 Therefore, as the elect of God, holy and beloved, put on tender mercies, kindness, humility, meekness, longsuffering;
> 13 bearing with one another, and forgiving one another, if anyone has a complaint against another; even as Christ forgave you, so you also must do.
> 14 But above all these things put on love, which is the bond of perfection.
> 15 And let the peace of God rule in your hearts, to which also you were called in one body; and be thankful. (NKJV)

These are statements of choice. If you had no choice, Paul would not have urged us to do these things. We would have done them only by the sovereignty of Our Heavenly Father and not needed any urging, suggesting, compelling, or other means to bring this to our attention. We have the choice. If you want to learn how to grow onions you should seek out a gardener who has expertise in growing onions. The gardener can provide you with vital information and steps to growing a successful onion. You will know when, how, and where to plant but the choice is yours. Paul embraced the revelation of Love just as he had previously embraced the Mosaic Law. Once he had his encounter with Jesus, the rest of the pieces to the puzzle had come into view. Love is the basis of the Law and without it only produces death. Paul was instructed by Our Heavenly Father to write two thirds of the New Testament. He urges us to embrace those truths that cause us to produce good fruit for the Kingdom as well as ourselves. He directs us toward the light and away from the darkness. Those that embrace these truths are the "elect of God". What a blessing to be one of the Elect and to be holy and beloved! What choices are we urged to make?

Put on tender mercies or clothe yourself with a heart of mercy. You have a choice to be merciful or judgmental. Which choice do you want Our Heavenly Father to make when dealing with your humanity? Do you want judgment raining down on you every time you screw up? Of course not. "Give, and it shall be given unto you; good measure, pressed down, and shaken together, and running over, shall men give into your bosom. For with the same measure that ye mete withal it shall be measured to you again." This truth is applicable to administering mercy or judgment to those who have sinned against you. You have the choice to promote the division created by the sin or restoration by exercising mercy toward the sinner. The choice is yours. However if you exercise judgment against the sinner, be prepared to receive judgment for your own sins. The seeds you sow are your choice, you are accountable. Paul understood this truth for he walked on the side of judgment and understood its ramifications.

Put on kindness. Why do people find it necessary to alienate themselves from others? Often it is the ego expressing a hurt that demands restitution so the person wants to bring attention to the injustice, but in a perverted way. "I've been messed around so I want everyone else to pay for it as well." "Life has not been fair to me so everyone must join me in my misery." The cycle just goes on. How can it be stopped? An act of kindness! Jesus died for the ungodly. Kindness does not demand the recipient to deserve it for kindness is unconditional. Acts of kindness diffuse the anger and animosity that have taken control of a person's life. It pierces that shell that has encompassed the person's life. Deep down people want to be loved and kindness is an outward expression of Love that shows the recipient you do care about him or her.

Put on humility. The word "humility" is often referred to as being lowly but it is more aptly referring to being moderate and not envious towards someone with apparently more. The status of an individual is relative to his or her environment. Someone making $25,000 in the U.S. is not wealthy whereas the same person with that salary in Romania would be in the upper echelon. Be content with where you are at. Seek Our Heavenly Father and you will rise to your calling and its associated resources. Our Heavenly Father resists the proud for they are never content with their station in life and are always comparing themselves to others with more resources. Resources do not bring peace, operating in your calling does.

You have the choice to have a heart of gratitude or to be ungrateful and miserable. Gratitude is a key to the heart for gratitude unlocks a revelation of Love that is otherwise hidden within the recesses of the heart. We take for granted so much around us. Our ego would have us believe that we are entitled to those aspects of life that seem minor to most people. Are you grateful for the air you breathe? If you lived around a coal mine in China where there is low air quality, you might have a greater appreciation for the air you breathe. Are you grateful for a good night's sleep? If you have ever had insomnia, you should thank Our Heavenly Father when you have received eight hours of sound, restful sleep. Your soul and body were at peace which allowed you to enjoy the rest. Many of us have prayed over our food. In decades past, the food may not have been as safe to eat and the prayer of nourishment may have been a heartfelt petition to cleanse the food of harmful bacteria. Why not express gratitude for the fact that you have this food? Why not be grateful for the finances to put the food on the table in the first place? Look out your window. Isn't there something to be grateful for right before your eyes?

Choose to become closer to Our Heavenly Father, but remember your motives will be judged. If you pursue Our Heavenly Father for any other reason but Love, judgment will arrive on your doorstep. In James chapter 4:

> 3 You ask and do not receive, because you ask amiss, that you may spend it on your pleasures.
> 4 Adulterers and adulteresses! Do you not know that friendship with the world is enmity with God? Whoever therefore wants to be a friend of the world makes himself an enemy of God. (NKJV)

In the Pentecostal faith movement, Christians were taught to acquire "things" by using various Scriptures as a demand for Our Heavenly Father to perform. That did not work! They were taught that if you claim a promise enough, Our Heavenly Father would ultimately reward you. Do you really think Our Heavenly Father would give in to such manipulation? What happened to the passage "Thy Will be done"? The key to faith is to first hear what Our Heavenly Father says, then believe! If HE says to believe HIM for your house to be paid off, then do it. Funds will come to you supernaturally and your mortgage will be paid in full. I know this from personal experience.

As we seek Our Heavenly Father's face, we will know what resources to ask for. We must never forget that HE created the earth to provide for all of the needs of mankind. HE did not forget anything essential to our wellbeing. HE is also well aware of our individuals needs and has the ability to bring forth anything we need for our calling and purpose. On the other hand, we must not think that Our Heavenly Father is our servant waiting to supply every whim based on our selfish demands. When we were as toddlers, HIS grace and mercy prevailed knowing that we knew no difference. But now we are to walk in maturity and realize the need for reverence in our lives. We now understand the magnitude of the privilege to be able to have such a relationship with the Creator of heaven and earth. Our immature demands have been replaced with mature desires to be of service and seek only those resources needful for our calling. Our Loving Father will then give us the desires of our hearts knowing that we will only draw closer to HIM.

Choose meekness. I always had a problem with the word "meekness" until I realized that it meant "moderation". We should live our lives in moderation. For those who live in moderation shall inherit the earth. Extravagance and excess feed the ego and once you start feeding the ego, you have unleashed a monster in your personal life. The ego strives for control and is the enemy of your spirit. It wants to consume all aspects of your life and when unbridled, it will lead to death and destruction. Drug addiction is a prime example of how a person can start with an innocent prescription and get a "taste" of euphoria and submit to its lure. Before long this person begins stealing from friends and family to feed the beast. They lose control and finally go to jail unless they die an unfortunate early death. The impact of this beast is widespread. A life of moderation will steer you away from the excesses brought on by drugs and alcohol.

Put on longsuffering or patience, endurance, constancy, steadfastness, perseverance. This fruit of the Spirit may be one of your best barometers in determining your spiritual maturity. Comprehending the sovereignty of Our Heavenly Father helps you appreciate that any situation or obstacle at hand is subject to change and will change in due time. Clearly if we had the certainty of knowing the future, we would have no need of longsuffering. If by the first of the month, we knew that a certain event would happen to change the circumstances, we would simply make a note on the calendar and go about our daily business. However, as we trust Our Heavenly Father and HIS plan for our lives we will walk in that same assurance as though we had been given a date for the obstacle to be removed. As we draw closer to Our Heavenly Father we perceive that assurance.

We should choose to be forbearing with one another, forgiving. Each of us has a unique history of experiences that affect our lives and thought processes. A person who is adopted views life with a slightly different perspective than someone raised by the birth parents. The ego would have the adopted child believe that he or she had something inherently wrong which caused the parents to reject the child. But as we begin to understand that Our Heavenly Father is the originator of our life and chose the parent to birth us, we will then gain comfort in that fact that there was no mistake made in our arrival. Our Heavenly Father was not surprised by the adoption but orchestrated the process to move the child into the path best suited for the development of the child's calling. Since the calling's preparation occurs over such a time span, we tend to become impatient in the development. Each of us is at a different stage of development and must be patient with others who have not progressed as quickly as we would expect. Their unique circumstances assure a unique time frame to maturity. We must be forbearing with others who are not as far along in their walk.

Isn't it time to do what matters? Many people go through life without considering what is truly important. Their focus is self-centered and as long as they are kept in a satisfied state, all is well. Laying up treasures in Heaven is not even on their radar. The lust of the eyes, the lust of the flesh, and/or the pride of life consumes them and their resources. What is your purpose? You must ask that question, your spirit demands an answer. Once you know your purpose or your calling, each day should guide you closer to the fulfillment. Yes, there will be days of rest and relaxation. Our Heavenly Father is not a taskmaster. But as we mature in our relationship with Our Heavenly Father, we will look forward to what each day brings. As we move toward the center of our individual callings, we will experience what it is like to be in the flow of HIS Spirit. We will see the connectedness of HIS Spirit with others. We will be prepared by the Spirit when we interact with those whose callings connect with ours. We are all connected in some fashion. There is no "nothingness" out there. We are not islands.

Procrastination is a choice, choosing to do nothing. That still, small voice tells us to take action or respond. What do you do? Do you take heed or do you respond "maybe another day". Delaying the inevitable only makes matters worse. As a steward of the gifts I have been given by My Heavenly Father, I must respond as a steward who loves to fulfill My Heavenly Father's desires. As I do, I enter into HIS rest and it is like being in the middle of a river and flowing with the river, enjoying the journey. It takes minimal energy to stay in the middle of the current. With a few minor corrections we can stay in the flow. But if we fail to react and delay our response, we could easily end up in the brush at the edge of the river, entangled in the cares of the world. Respond to the Spirit. Repent when you are urged to repent. Forgive when you are urged to forgive. Show up when you are summoned. As you are quick to respond to HIS Word, you are given more to steward over.

You can expect to be tested when you make the right choice. That is part of stewardship. When you choose to be a steward, you are given three things:

1. Responsibility and accountability
2. Time and resources
3. An adversary to test you

In the parable of the talents, each man was given a different amount of money to steward over. Each was given responsibility to go and do business. They were to manage their Lord's resources. Afterwards, the Lord left and they were given substantial time to go about and produce good fruit. After sufficient time had passed, the day of reckoning had arrived. Two of the stewards had passed the test and were rewarded. The third steward had failed. Why? He did not know the character of his Lord. He took the talent given to him and buried it.

Each of us is given a set of talents. Those talents will either be developed to produce fruit for the Kingdom or they will be buried in the recesses of our soul. It is our choice. Each of us will have an adversary or adversaries that will force us to choose what path we take. Will we be misdirected and take an alternate path? Will we be challenged as we walk on the right path only to give up when the pressure is applied? Our commitment is what is left after the emotion is worn off. Are you fully committed to your calling? Are you fully committed to the Kingdom of GOD? Your biggest adversary will be your ego. When other adversaries depart, your ego is still there and wanting to control your every move and your every thought. Love is stronger than any ego. Love will take command as you choose to walk in Love even when confronted by your enemies. Death has no sting when you walk in Love. What can your enemy really do to you if you no longer love the world and its trappings?

Love overcomes all adversaries. Jesus overcame death by resurrection and we have been given that same power by His blood. We must choose to embrace the fullness of the power from On High. However, this power is highly protected and can only be accessed through the Door of Love and with a key. David knew this and pursued the Heart of Our Heavenly Father. As we choose to immerse ourselves in HIS Love we will gain access to that power. We will become the good stewards who enter into The Rest. We will know the character of Our Lord, do business, and bring forth good fruit. Thy Kingdom come, Thy Will be done!

Personal Assessment:
1. Have you chosen to walk in Love?
2. Do you start the day contemplating what acts of Love you can accomplish?
3. Do you end the day with an assessment of your successes and failures in your Love walk?
4. Are you becoming immediately conscious of your ego's attempt to maintain control?
5. Does your checkbook reflect your choice of Love?

Chapter 18
LOVE COMPELS

"For the love of Christ compels us..."

Why do we do the things we do? What is our motivation? Why did I spend the countless hours writing this book? The Love of Christ compels me to write and share the burning revelation of HIS Love and the fruit thereof.

The prophets of old could be viewed as having an axe to grind. They seemed to be the purveyors of bad news. How often did one of them arrive to say "Good job!"? However they were compelled by the Love of Christ to speak prophetically to the people so that they might repent or turn from their wicked ways. Yes, it was unpopular to tell people of their impending doom yet one of the greatest sacrifices of Love is to through yourself in harm's way for your brother, the stranger, and even your personal enemy.

If a father sees his son heading for destruction, does he remain silent and allow the son to destroy himself because of some foolish, immature act? Certainly not! If after four decades of pursuing the heart of Our Heavenly Father I find a revelation that exceeds all the other revelations and I believe that this revelation provides the key to the entrance to Heaven, should I remain silent?

Throughout Scripture men have taken bold steps based solely on the revelation they received from Above. Abraham was willing to sacrifice his son based on his faith that he heard from Heaven. Moses overcame insurmountable odds to take a group of slaves and their families out of the richest nation on earth into an unknown land. Joshua was compelled to take on thirty-one kings in order to conquer the land. Mary was approached to do the seemingly impossible- have a baby without knowing a man.

Each of us is given the opportunity to step out in faith based on our personal belief that we have heard a Divine Word from Heaven specifically for us. Sometimes we need a confirming sign, maybe two or three. But in the end we are compelled to move forward. Within our hearts we know this compelling force is somehow tied to our purpose. We just can't help it at times. Just as a thoroughbred colt is born to run, we must act in response to this compelling force that operates inside of us. It resides in each of us even though there have been many who have done their best to suppress it. We have been created with this need for the Love of Christ to be resident in us. Those who have rejected this Love will become acquainted with it at some time in the future, for every knee shall bow and every tongue confess that Jesus Christ is Lord.

What about now? Are you compelled by the Love of Christ or are you walking in the ego-centric, entitled attitude that the world promotes? Slogans such as "you deserve a break today" and "everyone has a right to own a house" promote this sense of entitlement. As we mature in our walk with Our Heavenly Father we will appreciate the life HE has given us. We will pay attention to all of the various aspects of life that make up this universe. Our attention to detail will be sensitized and our gratitude for the small things in life will come to the surface. Our prayer over the food we eat will become an expression of gratitude rather than simply a duty or tradition that has lost meaning.

The future awaits the "Love of Christ" to spread throughout the globe. Men have attempted to take the Throne of Our Heavenly Father and occupy it by actions of futility. They were only exalted in their minds and lived a life of deception and illusion. Our Heavenly Father was not moved by their attempts to replace HIM. The Creator is always greater than the created.

Countless recitals of the Lord's Prayer have prophesied of the Kingdom of GOD coming to earth. Men, women, and children have all recited this prophecy in unison. The earth has been put on notice as the Love of Christ is compelling men and women to rise up above the worldly path. The quest for revelation has at times been misdirected in an apparent attempt to slow the progression towards the goal of the full expression of the Kingdom of GOD on earth. Do you think any misdirection was unexpected by Our Heavenly Father? By necessity the revelation of Salvation needed to come forth first. We had to have a Savior in order to be saved. The Love of Christ started out as a seed and expressed itself on the Cross. That seed had to die in order to bring forth life. The Law of seedtime and harvest would be honored. Rather than be an exception to the Laws of Our Heavenly Father, the path of the Love of Christ would be an expression of the Law. The endgame of the Law is restoration and reconciliation, not death and destruction. The Love of Christ propels us toward life.

As children of the Most High GOD embrace the revelation of Love, they will be compelled to fulfill their purpose. They will shed the weights of the world that previously beset them. Their resources accumulated over time will become subject to the Love of Christ. As this happens the fear of scarcity will depart. This Scripture in Acts 2 will come alive:

> 44 Now all who believed were together, and had all things in common,
> 45 and sold their possessions and goods, and divided them among all, as anyone had need. (NKJV)

Are you willing to give up any of your resources for the Kingdom of GOD? I must say that this is the true test of where each of us is at. I am not promoting any action that prevents you from meeting your existing obligations for we are called to be good stewards. We don't give away our rent money unless Our Heavenly Father has specifically spoken and directed such an action. In that case, HE will provide the rent money. However, we must ask the question of what resources we have that should be directed for establishing the Kingdom. If this area puts you in a defensive mode, you are not being compelled by the Love of Christ. Love does not get offended. Yes, we have all been exploited by men who wanted us to fund their vision. Even noble intentions are temporal in the final analysis…

Each of us is wired internally to move towards Love. Our ego would cause us to resist and subdue that magnetic attraction to our ordained calling. The ego would attempt to bury your calling to the point of extinction if it could. Your calling is like DNA in that you have that encoding which cannot be erased for it is at the core of your existence. No matter how dormant your calling becomes it can be activated in a nanosecond. Our soul yearns for that calling to be released so that the fruit can express itself. Our purpose is the only thing that can bring us to full peace within ourselves. Until that peace arrives, we will be searching for something that will fulfill the void within us. You can mask the reality of who you are but it will ultimately surface at some point. Until then you will experience lost opportunity associated with the blessings of your calling.

Deep within us is the need to repent or turn back to the Face of Our Heavenly Father. Our ego would have us reside in darkness, yes even the outer darkness. The less we can perceive of spiritual things, the better for our ego. Yet Love will pierce that outer darkness when those who are called bring forth the message of "repentance". Repentance is not just for the extreme ungodly but also for those who have become lukewarm in their walk. The angel in Revelations spoke forth this reality:

> 15 "I know your works, that you are neither cold nor hot. I could wish you were cold or hot.
> 16 So then, because you are lukewarm, and neither cold nor hot, I will vomit you out of My mouth.
> 17 Because you say, 'I am rich, have become wealthy, and have need of nothing'—and do not know that you are wretched, miserable, poor, blind, and naked. (NKJV)

Money does not make you holy, special, or entitled. Actually, it often causes you more difficulty in matters of spiritual significance. Wealthy people have a tendency to spend their time and energy attempting to maintain or grow their wealth at the expense of their calling. They have forgotten those times when they had no money and could exist on much less. They have built their sandcastles expecting them to survive as permanent structures. Our Heavenly Father views money as a commodity. It is simply a tool to promote exchange of goods and services. It is a transporter of value. It converts time to tradable value.

Our Creator Who is the full expression of Love created every aspect of our being. Each particle has at its origin, Love. Every living thing was created with the same primal intent. Love is not a conditional action but the true reality of life. If we are not operating in Love it is due to blockages to that reality. Illusions would have us believe that this is not the case. As an aspect of HIS Love, Our Heavenly Father gives us the choice to live in the illusions or in the essence of Love, our true character. Yes, we were made in HIS likeness of Love.

Most of us enjoy amusement parks that entertain our illusions of being a super hero or defying gravity and speed. Those escapes of reality are fine as long as we do not fully embrace the illusion they represent and create a further blockage, suppressing Love to a greater degree. Submitting to Love steers us away from illusions that would take us further from the truth. Shedding those weights which easily beset us allow us to become more sensitive to Love's directives. Love compels us to no longer judge others but to see them as Our Heavenly Father sees them. They may be struggling with removal of their own illusions and blockages and we should not add to them but be a light to the reality of Love.

As you are being led by Love, your joy will dramatically increase. You will have that peace and assurance of your path towards the fullness of your calling. As John points out in 1 John:

> 3 that which we have seen and heard we declare to you, that you also may have fellowship with us; and truly our fellowship is with the Father and with His Son Jesus Christ.
> 4 And these things we write to you that your joy may be full. (NKJV)

Your joy is a great indicator of the state of your walk in Love. How much joy do you have? If there is none, your ego has you walking around with the burdens of the world strapped to your shoulders. Your adversary would have you believe those burdens are necessary for you to carry and that there is no one else to take on those weights. In many cases those burdens might be the focus of another person's calling and you are simply in the way and preventing that calling from coming to fruition. One man's drudgery is another man's delight. Some men hate doing yard work whereas I enjoy the opportunity to spend time in the backyard and observe nature while I am planting flowers or mowing the grass. Joy allows you to do the most mundane tasks with a new outlook. Joy is a fruit of Love. As you fellowship with Our Heavenly Father and Our Lord Jesus Christ, your joy will increase to a fullness that you have not experienced before. Both joy and peace are found in fellowshipping with Love. Your soul yearns for that joy and peace for they are the outworking of the Love within you. Removal of bondages allow those fruit to come forth just as removing a large rock from the flower bed allows the seeds that lay dormant to spring forth in beauty and fragrance.

Love compels us to break out of our bubble. Our ego would have us develop a comfort zone or a bubble to reside in. This bubble is designed to restrict our movements and rob us of opportunities to express Love to those in dire straits. We try to isolate ourselves from the unknown thinking that death and destruction are always lurking around the corner. Instead, as we walk in fellowship with Our Heavenly Father He will guide our steps away from the bubble created by our illusions. We will then experience greater joy as we interact with new acquaintances who need ministered that special word of Love which will begin to draw out the Love within them. In turn they will respond to Love by becoming an expression of Love as well. Those fictions created by the ego will no longer rule the thoughts and restrict the movements of that person you ministered to because your expression of Love broke through that bubble with the ease of a surgeon's scalpel. The Love contained within that person was simply waiting for the opportunity to surface and express itself once again.

The protective bubble was not prepared for the reality of Love to be on the outside trying to connect with the same Love contained within. This reality is the basis of the Kingdom of GOD overtaking the earth as it is in Heaven. As Love connects through those who return to the source of life, shedding the illusions, an interconnected net will form throughout the earth. This net will metaphorically be a similar net that caught the one hundred fifty-three fishes in the Book of John. Not one fish will be lost and the net will not break. Just as Love commanded those fish to give themselves as meat for the disciples, Love is commanding us to give of ourselves for mankind. Our agendas independent of Love will no longer matter.

Love compels us to become the ultimate sacrifice for others. Jesus made this clear in the following passage:

> John 10:15 As the Father knows Me, even so I know the Father; and I lay down My life for the sheep. (NKJV)

Love compelled Jesus to lose His life so that mankind could be restored to Our Heavenly Father. He opted not to use His power and authority to take the earthly throne offered to Him by the adversary and initially expected by the disciples. Instead He needed to be offered up as the sacrifice for mankind. Love fully assured Him of resurrection and restoration to Our Heavenly Father. The illusion of death would have no hold over His decision to go to the cross. His decision benefited every man, woman, and child to ever inhabit the earth. If Jesus Christ is our example, shouldn't we be willing to be a sacrifice as well? No, we do not need to go to the cross to bear all men's sins but we should be willing to give ourselves completely to Our Heavenly Fathers' wishes. Those illusions brought about by fear must be dealt with. We are constantly encouraged to "fear not" in Scripture. Our Loving Heavenly Father is not some distant creator unaware of our most intimate needs but He is available to supply all our needs according to the calling we are ordained to carry out. However, He is not obligated to sustain or promote our illusions. Jesus was well aware of the need to lose that life based on illusion when He spoke:

Matthew 10:39 "He who finds his life will lose it, and he who loses his life for My sake will find it. (NKJV)

Are you willing to lose your life for HIS sake? Love says "Yes" but the ego says "No". Your fear of loss comes from the illusion that this physical life is all there is, eternity does not does not exist. Love provides the wisdom, understanding, and assurance of your eternal existence. Love exposes the deception of immature thinking based on carnal thinking and assumptions. You have been given many experiences in life to expose this immature thinking. Simple observations of nature reconfirm what Love is compelling you to do. Lose your life and you will find it! Don't let those falsehoods rule your life for one more day. Turn back to the face of Our Heavenly Father and declare "Here I am Father, use me!" No longer deny your gifts and calling but let them spring forth.

Love compels us to live a merciful life. Judge not lest ye be judged. Such a simple statement has such great ramifications attached to it. The first thing that happens when you begin to walk in Love, your commitment will be challenged. You will be given the opportunity to judge someone who has become your adversary. Your character will be attacked and most likely the attack will be based on a lie. You will be tested in order to reveal what is in your heart: Love or judgment. This will become your barometer of your progress towards walking in Love. When you no longer lash out at your enemy but show compassion, you will experience joy over the change occurring inside of you. Your pride is being stripped away. You no longer have to impress anyone. Your sense of entitlement has been replaced with a servant's heart. You look to minister to others rather than attempting to extract something which they possess that would satisfy your ego and perpetuate its stronghold.

Love compels us to greatness in the Kingdom but it is done in a fashion that defies the world's logic, you must become as a child. Jesus reveals this in Matthew 18:

1 At that time the disciples came to Jesus, saying, "Who then is greatest in the kingdom of heaven?"
2 Then Jesus called a little child to Him, set him in the midst of them,
3 and said, "Assuredly, I say to you, unless you are converted and become as little children, you will by no means enter the kingdom of heaven.
4 Therefore whoever humbles himself as this little child is the greatest in the kingdom of heaven.
5 Whoever receives one little child like this in My name receives Me. (NKJV)

Jesus speaks about two different aspects of Heaven in the above passage: entrance and greatness. To enter Heaven you must first convert from what you have become. Jesus was speaking to adults who have grown in experience and the world's logic. Jesus said you must become as a child who has none of the world's logic or experience to draw upon. Instead the child perceives the world through innocent eyes. The child calls "a spade a spade" and does not mince words with prepackaged, well thought out rhetoric designed to manipulate or control the situation. The child simply and innocently tells it like it is with no judgment or malice attached. We are called to the same innocent perception without judgment. We are called to observe reality for what it is without attempting to add or subtract anything from it. Reality does not need our commentary about some prophetic sign that may or may not be there. If it is to be a sign to us Our Heavenly Father will let us know. Otherwise just observe reality and enjoy what it is trying to communicate to us. As we become like little children we will begin to notice the beauty of reality that our logic and ego has blinded us from since our childhood. Our ego will attempt to restrain us from converting to innocent perception but Love compels us to return to that purity.

The second aspect is greatness but it only occurs after we convert to the innocence. We must walk in humbleness. You must be willing to become a servant to mankind and shed that attitude of entitlement.

Ascending to Love

You must be willing to stand at the back rather than vie for the front. You must prefer your brother over yourself. You must be willing to invest in others' lives rather than seeking your own. You must be guided by the power of Love in your heart rather than your mind for innocence is found only in the heart. By converting to the innocence of a child, Love will compel you toward abundance, not scarcity. You will begin to behold the infinite universe and its fruits. The trappings of the world will lose their appeal to you. You will seek ways to help others rather than seek ways to exploit their gifts for your benefit. Being motivated and compelled by Love will draw you toward greatness in the Kingdom of GOD. As this conversion takes place, your joy will return to you as will the other fruit of the Spirit.

As your conversion to the child-like innocent perception proceeds, you will begin to embrace the positive and disregard the negative. As you feed your mind with the positive, it will become positive and will behave in a positive fashion. Your mind will become your servant rather than your master. It records and collects what you expose it to. As this occurs your awareness increases and the blindness is lifted from your eyes. Creativity replaces cynicism. Your limitations of imagination are lifted and you are now ready to bring forth new fruit to feed mankind. Rather than the downward spiral created by death and destruction, you are now being propelled to the higher realms of existence and moving towards a closer relationship with Our Heavenly Father. Your eyes will be filled with compassion rather than condescension. Small children will look at you and perceive the Love emanating from your being. They will be drawn to you rather than being frightened of you. Nature embraces the Love that created it and it will respond and be drawn to you. Contradictions contained in your mind will evaporate. You will cease to be in conflict with life and instead embrace life to the fullest.

As you embrace the Love of Christ you will experience Heaven on earth. The reality of Love will overtake your soul and you will enter into the fullness of your calling. You will ascend to new heights in Love and all that you have been called to accomplish will come to pass. This is the purpose of this book!

Personal Assessment:
1. Have you seen your purpose and your focus place a greater emphasis on the Love walk after reading this book?
2. Is there someone you know that would benefit from reading and discussing each chapter of this book on a weekly basis?
3. Are you committed to serving mankind to a greater degree now?
4. Are "things" truly becoming less important in your life?
5. Go into the world and let people see Our Heavenly Father in your face.